TIGER WRITING

The WILLIAM E. MASSEY SR. LECTURES *in the* HISTORY OF AMERICAN CIVILIZATION 2012

GISH JEN

TIGER WRITING

ART, CULTURE, AND THE
INTERDEPENDENT SELF

Harvard University Press

Cambridge, Massachusetts

London, England

2013

Grateful acknowledgment is made for permission to
reprint an excerpt from the following copyrighted
song: "Helplessness Blues," words and music by Robin
Pecknold. © 2011 Foxes Fellowship (ASCAP).

Library of Congress Cataloging-in-Publication Data
Jen, Gish.
    Tiger Writing : Art, Culture, and the Interdependent
Self / Gish Jen.
        pages cm.—(The William E. Massey Sr. Lectures in
the History of American Civilization)
    Includes bibliographical references and index.
    ISBN 978-0-674-07283-1 (alk. paper)
    1. Jen, Gish.   2. Novelists, American—Biography.
3. Narration (Rhetoric).   4. Fiction—Authorship.
5. Self-actualization (Psychology).   I. Title.
    PS3560.E474Z46   2013
    813´.54—dc23   2012043631
    [B]

For Werner Sollors

On behalf of the many he has inspired and heartened,

with respect and gratitude

CONTENTS

Author's Note   ix

Introduction   1

1   My Father Writes His Story   11

2   Art, Culture, and Self   57

3   What Comes of All That   103

Notes 163   Works Cited 177
Index 187

Author's Note

I am a novelist. I do not normally lecture. But a year and a half ago, the chairman of Harvard's Program in the History of American Civilization, John Stauffer, asked me if I would give a series of three lectures the program hosts each year called the Massey Lectures; and to this invitation, I said yes. I said yes not just because I was so honored—although, of course, I was—but because I knew that despite thirty years of writing novels, stories, and articles, there was something in my bones I had not quite managed to articulate—a special way in which my cultural background was profoundly at odds with the literary culture I negotiated every day.

This was especially on my mind because my father, a Chinese immigrant, had recently written a personal history I found at once completely familiar and completely baffling. Why did he write so much about his house? I wondered. Why did he not write more about himself? But also it was on my mind because, as I began to understand how to read his narrative, I saw that the self it reflected was a self I saw in the news all the time, and a self that was often greeted, as I had greeted my father's, with bafflement. What's more, it was, I was coming to realize, a part of my own self.

These lectures—the result of that bafflement—are, first and foremost, about art and culture. However, the artistic disconnect they describe between East and West sheds light, as it happens, on the everyday narratives of many corners of the world—most recently, for example, Cairo. There, after the storming of the U.S. Embassy, many in America wondered how the protesters could be more upset about a stupid video made by a stupid man than, say, about the killing of Muslims in hate crimes. To this one Egyptian, quoted in the *New York Times,* answered, "When you hurt someone, you are just hurting one person . . . But when you insult a faith like that, you are insulting a whole nation that feels the pain." As if that were an explanation, some of us might grumble, even as a part of us might wonder, as I did, whether this way of putting things together wasn't related to why the Chinese, too, can be thin-skinned and nationalistic? And was this in turn related to why Asian American test scores are so high?

I am grateful beyond measure to have been given an occasion to pull together the mix of memoir, cognitive studies, literary analysis, and reflection that was involved in answering these questions, and in getting that "something in my bones" out onto the page. It is a something that I myself found revelatory to explore, and a something that I am now hoping will speak to people both in and beyond the literary world. I must confess that in connection with it, I also talk a bit about my own work and how I became a writer. This is because John Stauffer had hinted that an intellectual autobiography might be nice, and because several of my early readers had seconded him at high volume. I do hope I have not ruined the lectures by complying.

In any case, I thank with all my heart the many people who made this magpie work possible. My list starts with John Stauffer and the Massey Lecture committee, whose invitation still amazes me, if I think about it. Among the wonders of the live lectures were John's most able lecture summaries, as well as the graceful and extraordinarily generous introductions given by Nancy Cott, Ju Yon Kim, and Amanda Claybaugh. My thanks go, too, to the legions of behind-the-scenes elves who worked so hard to make everything run smoothly, especially Chief Elf, Arthur Patton-Hock.

I am more beholden than I can say to the many wise and perceptive readers who reviewed early drafts of this project, including Eileen Cheng-yin Chow, David Damrosch, Patricia Greenfield, Bill Marx, Allyssa McCabe, Martha Minow, Werner Sollors, and my mother, Agnes Jen. Thanks as well to the dozens of patient friends who answered with precision and provocation my innumerable questions. And let me say that the fact there is now a written version of these talks poised to enter the world is very much due to the untiring efforts of my agent, Melanie Jackson, and her assistant, Katherine Chen, as well as those of the warm and enterprising crew at Harvard University Press, including Lindsay Waters, Shan Wang, Kate Brick, Margaux Leonard, Lisa Roberts, and Greg Kornbluh.

My greatest debt of all will forever be to my father, Norman Chao-pe Jen, whose words and spirit animate much more than just these lectures; it was a supremely special pleasure to be able to deliver them in his presence. I salute, too, with love, my husband, David O'Connor, and my children, Luke and Paloma, for their lifesaving humor, patience, and support. As for the many colleagues, friends, neighbors, students, and strangers who came from far and near to attend the lectures—I will remember you all my days.

And now off with these words—*send!* May they make some sense and do some good.

October 14, 2012
Cambridge, Massachusetts

TIGER WRITING

INTRODUCTION

A couple of years ago I attended an East-West literary conference, over the course of which a young mainland Chinese writer was asked why she wrote.[1] To this she answered, not to tell stories, or to bear witness, or to be in sacred communion with Jane Austen, but rather that she wrote because she did not like to go out, and thought that by writing novels she could make money and stay home. To which all I could think was, *Oy!*—which was just Yiddish for what I suspect many of the Westerners in the audience were thinking.

And you know, I have been thinking about this ever since—this question of why, when we in the West think of writers who like to stay home, we think *Emily Dickinson* and *Art* (capital A), whereas the Chinese are perfectly capable of thinking *Convenience* (capital C). Last winter, for example, I met a woman who is organizing a rocket to take works of art up into space. This is part of a contest whose point, she said, is for "the worlds beyond our earth to receive human-made works of beauty." An amazing project, I think you'll agree, and one to which my first reaction was, *A rocket! What fun!* but my second, *Now here is something that only an American would be doing*—this person's attitude toward the value and purpose of human expression being quite different than that of the Chinese writer, and the difference between them, I would argue, representing the tip of a very large iceberg.

In inviting me to give these lectures, John Stauffer suggested that I consider an intellectual autobiography—a polite way of suggesting, perhaps, that I address the one and only subject on which I am a worldwide expert, namely myself. That, though, could still mean a great many things; and so it is that I have chosen to use my own case as a way of talking about the aforementioned iceberg. I will not be able to map it definitively in our short time together. Still, via my own story, I plan to talk a bit about both culture with a small c and Culture with a large, with a particular focus on different constructions of the self. By this I mean the independent, individualistic self that dominates in the West, especially America, and the interdependent, collectivist self that dominates in the East, including China, from whence my parents emigrated in the 1940s.

I have been interested in this difference for a while. In talking a few weeks ago to my old teacher from the Iowa Writers' Workshop, James Alan McPherson, I was reminded that it was the subject of the essay I wrote in conjunction with my master's thesis in 1983. And if I look back over the novels that followed, I can see that if I have embodied a dialectic, as some writers do, it is the tension scholar Werner Sollors has so pithily put as between consent and descent, which in my case is also a struggle between Emerson and Confucius. I think we all feel this tension to a degree: between an independent self that finds meaning in the truth within, and to whom rights and self-expression are important; and an interdependent self that finds meaning in affiliation, and duty, and self-sacrifice. That is to say that if we think of Hamlet's assertion, "I have that within me that passes show," we resonate, feeling that we, too, have something in us that others can't see, and to which we must "above all be true."[2] Yet if we think of the end of *Casablanca,* when Humphrey Bogart says, "the problems of three little people don't amount to a hill of beans in this crazy world," we find we resonate as well.

My tension is simply a more extreme version of this. Thanks to globalization, it is also one whose acuteness is shared by more all the time, what with the difference in self typically thought of as East–West actually being, as psychologist Richard Nisbett notes, between the "West and the rest"—with "the West" here referring to Europe and North America, and "the rest" referring to the rest of the world; and what with accelerating modernization now bringing to "the rest" a veritable epidemic of individualism. I should probably say here that to the extent that I bring cross-cultural studies into these lectures—as I will especially in the first half of the second lecture—I will keep to various East–West findings—that focus being, as I think you'll agree, quite broad enough. Still, what with the traditionally interdependent but now fluctuating orientation of many African, Middle Eastern, and Latin American cultures, not to say numerous European and American subcultures, there are more and more people like me every day—changelings, often usefully able to tap into our inter- or independent selves as the situation warrants, but connoisseurs of a certain dissonance, too. As for what sort of children we changeling adults will raise, who knows? And what their children will be, and their children's children, is obviously impossible to say. But in any case, in describing, over the next few days, some of the ironies and gifts of my own experience, I hope to bring perspective not only to the enterprise of novel-writing, but to the experiences of many with no particular connection to literature.

Before I begin, I'd like to say that with this, as with all discussions involving cultural difference, I am aware of the danger of stereotyping. "Simplistic and overexaggerated beliefs about a group, generally acquired second-hand and resistant to change," as sociologist Martin M. Marger put it, are obviously to be roundly condemned and absolutely avoided. I am also aware, though, that fear of stereotyping has sometimes led to a discomfort with any assertion of cultural difference, no matter how thoroughly accepted by psychologists or how firmly grounded in research. This concern is, sadly, altogether reasonable. In his 1932 classic, *Remembering*, psychologist Frederic C. Bartlett describes an experiment in which British test subjects were asked to repeatedly retell a Native American ghost tale after intervals that ranged from a matter of minutes to a matter of months. The results were revealing: with each new round, the subjects misremembered yet more, unconsciously editing and reshaping the tale—changing seal hunting to "fishing," for example, and removing and altering what seemed to them weird story elements—until it had become something no longer Native American at all—until it had become, in fact, pretty bloody British.

Existing schema are powerful. We hear the expected far better than the unexpected and recall things in light of what we already think. And should we doubt that even the best of us is capable of irrationally defending our schema, novelist Alan Lightman reminds us that the likes of Einstein and Max Planck have been known to defend theirs in the face of opposing evidence. So when we are dense, we do have good company. At the same time, tendencies are only tendencies. Though these lectures may well be misconstrued and misremembered, I hold out hope that they will not—that they will not be filtered so much as they will draw attention to our filters, and that this will ultimately foster constructive conversation.

A note about terminology: I have not used the word "independent" as it is popularly used, to mean self-sufficient or free from outside control; neither have I used the word "interdependent" to mean interconnected or mutually dependent. Rather I have used these words as cross-cultural psychologists do, as a way of describing two very different models of self-construal. The first—the "independent," individualistic self—stresses uniqueness, defines itself via inherent attributes such as its traits, abilities, values, and preferences, and tends to see things in isolation. The second—the "interdependent," collectivist self—stresses commonality, defines itself via its place, roles, loyalties, and duties, and tends to see things in context.[3] Naturally, between these two very different self-construals lies a continuum along which most people are located, and along which they may move, too, over the course of their lives or even over the course of a moment. Culture is not fate; it only offers templates, which individuals can finally accept, reject, or modify, and do. For example, true as it clearly is that Americans love cars, many people don't drive, or don't drive much, or don't like what driving does to the environment, or find that cars make them carsick.

At the same time, ours is indisputably a car culture, with the fact of the car influencing everything from our city design to our foreign policy. And so it is with the inter-/independence spectrum. Wherever along its length people typically situate themselves, and however widely they tend to range, its endpoints nonetheless represent influential cultural realities—realities that give rise, as we shall see, to profoundly different ways of perceiving, remembering, and narrating both self and world. My ultimate focus in exploring these will be on the role of their difference in the spawning and sustaining of my writing life. However, as I have suggested, this difference has implications far beyond that—for our understanding of art and of the novel, for our understanding of ourselves, and for our understanding of culture and of cultural change, which is to say of the world in which we live.

As for my plan of action, we will begin with a "roots" lecture that is also an example of how an interdependent self might narrate a life. That is to say that we will be looking at the opening of a wonderful autobiography my father wrote when he was eighty-five. This section is about growing up in China—a bit of writing that I hope will move and interest us, but also ground us, supplying the sort of feel for interdependence that we cannot get from studies alone.

Not that we will deprive ourselves of studies. In

the first half of the second lecture we will in fact turn, as I mentioned, to a number of studies in cross-cultural psychology as a way of deepening our understanding of my father's story. They will also give us insight into its opposite, that highly independent enterprise, Western narrative, on which we will focus in the second half of the lecture. Here we will be looking at the relationship between culture with a small c and Culture with a large, and what all this has to do with my beginnings as a writer.

Then, in the third lecture, we will consider what comes of all we have been discussing besides a migraine. What happens when interdependence meets independence? I will be setting myself and my work in this unsettled context, as well as the work of others, and paying a visit, besides, to a most unorthodox engineering classroom.

As for my plans for after that, they are to spend the day in a hot tub. But first: art, culture, and the interdependent self.

1

MY FATHER WRITES HIS STORY

In 2005, when he was eighty-five, my father sat down to write his life story.[1] This begins simply: "It is few days before my 86th birthday. I am writing my personal history for my family." As for what follows, it is notably un-self-centered. Written over the period of a month and totaling thirty-two pages, it does not begin à la David Copperfield with "I was born"; in what we will come to recognize as true interdependent style, my father does not, in fact, mention his birth at all. We do not hear how much he weighed or whether he peed on the nurse, much less anything remotely like "the clock began to strike, and I began to cry, simultaneously." In fact, he does not even give his birth date until page eight, when he includes "Norman Chao-Pe Jen, June 26, 1919" in conjunction with another event, and in parentheses.[2]

Instead he begins: "(1) Ancient History," drawing his information from his family genealogy book. This is an item those of you who have read my novel *The Love Wife* will recognize as the bait with which Carnegie Wong's mother, Mama Wong, gets Carnegie to take in a woman who appears to be a second wife. It is the sort of genealogical record that was traditionally kept by any family who could afford to do so, and was of course always prized—but never more so than now, what with every book that survived the Cultural Revolution having done so by a miracle. Cellist Yo-Yo Ma's family genealogy book, for example, long hidden inside a wall, was found during a home renovation; and my mother's was found when Shanghai families whose things had been confiscated during the Cultural Revolution were allowed inside a warehouse with the idea that if you could find what was taken from you, you could reclaim it. I don't think you have to be a novelist to imagine the piles of stuff, and the crowds and the chaos, and the despair with which people like my aunts pored over the heaps. Finally, though, my youngest aunt simply stopped and, closing her eyes, prayed to our ancestors to help; and when she opened her eyes and turned around, right there, at eye level, was the family genealogy book.

My father's family was less lucky; the physical

book itself did not survive. At least one copy, though, did, thanks to the Japanese, who for reasons perhaps related to their use of the Jen family compound as their regional headquarters during their occupation of China, preserved one in a Japanese library. This served as the basis for an unofficial update, done by a Taiwan relative. But in any case, my father, drawing upon genealogical charts like the one shown on the next page, begins:

(1) Ancient History

Chinese history book indicated that about 4,000 years ago, one of the Emperor's . . . wi[v]e[s] gave birth [to] two sons. The Emperor was happy [and gave] the last name of "Jen" to his two sons. To-day we recognize them as first generation of cycle I[.]

These two sons and their descendants lived in Shandong [province] for many years. One [of] their descendants [in the] 69th generation move[d] away to Shanxi [province]. He started . . . [the] first generation of cycle 2. Some of their descendants moved to Henan, but [still cycle 2] continued . . . for 78 generation[s].

By the year . . . 1131 which was [in the] South Song Dynasty and 874 years before 2005, Some of [the Shanxi Jens moved] to [the town of] yi-Xing [and] started [the] first generation of cycle 3. My grandfather [belonged to the 26th] generation . . . of cycle 3. My father was 27th [generation] and myself is 28th generation.

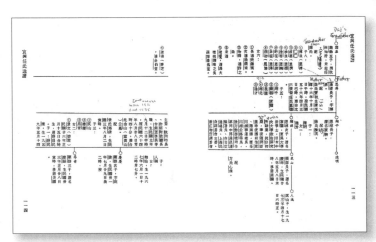

A chart from the update of the Jen family genealogical book

Of course, it is a bit hard for us in the West to imagine that a family should even think to claim to trace its ancestry back 4,500 years to Huángdì, the legendary Yellow Emperor who founded Chinese civilization. To trace your family back to the *Mayflower* is one thing; this is more like tracing your family to Adam and Eve. It is, however, not an uncommon way for Chinese genealogies to begin. As for how accurate the older records are, who knows. The Yíxīng genealogy of the last twenty-eight generations, though—the 874 years before my father sat down to write this personal history—is apparently correct.

Not that historical accuracy exactly matters for our purposes, since you may gather in any case how deeply tied up our sense of family is with place. Of course, things have changed for us as for many Chinese families. My siblings and I were born in America, and not long ago I heard a Malaysian in-law say, "Home is where the job is." And yet I think it fair to say that when the Chinese talk about their hometowns—the word for which is literally "old home," *lăojiā*—they are talking about an association difficult to fathom in peripatetic America. Traditionally, your hometown meant everything—interweave that it was of your physical context, your historical context, and your relational context; and a certain density of weave being common in China. Your place in the family, for example, was often worked into your name, which could in turn, as in my father's case, be worked into the house. That may be a little hard for us to get, but after the summary of the generations, my father explains it, saying:

My grand father's house [had eight words] posted . . . on the door[s]. These 8 words . . . [provided] the middle names for the following 8 generations. My grand father has the first word. My father has the second word and my middle name is the third word.

That is to say that there were eight characters posted on the doors that faced one of the house's courtyards. The source of these eight characters was a couplet the emperor gave our family, *Guó ēn jiā qìng,*

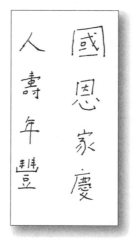

The couplet, written out by my mother

Rén shòu nián fēng, which might be loosely translated, "May the emperor grant us favor, May the family celebrate, May everyone live a long time, and May the year bring a good harvest." A bit of officialese, one suspects. And yet it was taken quite seriously by my great grandfather and used to reify the interdependence of our family, with the middle name of every male Jen drawn from it, and with all the men of each generation bearing the same name. For example, the names of all the males in my father's generation have the word *jiā* in them. (My father's "official" name is Rén Jiā Zòu.)[3] The names of all the males in my generation similarly include the word *qīng*,[4] and though, thanks to the traditional sexism, neither my Chinese name nor my sister's follows suit,[5] I am happy to report that my daughter, Kāng Rén Mǐn, does have a generation name, *rén*, like her brother, Kāng Rén Yào. As for what happens when my great-great-grandchildren reach the end of the couplet, my understanding is that they simply start at the beginning again. And as for the first names that go with the generation names, I have recently been thinking of having my parents draw some up the way my great-grandfather used to do. Supporting some of what I will be claiming in these lectures about the relative de-emphasizing of uniqueness in the East, my great-grandfather reportedly used to have a little wine and then just sit and make up names he liked. When children were born, they were assigned the next name on the list.

My father, in any case, using the couplet to organize his narrative, follows his introduction with a section about the generation named after the first character, *guó*—his grandfather's generation. He devotes the next section to the generation named after the second character, *ēn*—his father's generation— and so on. This is an organization that would actually make sense even independent of the couplet, since the granting of the couplet was to begin with a recognition of my father's grandfather's status. He was, after all, the one who put this branch of the family on the map—the one who made its fortune, built its compound, and in many ways defined the edenic years of peace and prosperity my father enjoyed in Yíxīng.

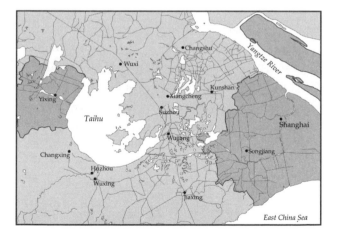

A map of the Shanghai area, showing Yíxīng.

Today Yíxīng is a place you can find easily enough on Google Maps. For me, though, growing up in the days when China was "closed," it was as legendary as Babylon or Troy. It lies in Jiangsu province, just west of Shanghai, on the west shore of Tàihú—Lake Tai—the third largest freshwater lake in China, and a lake that I always imagined as timeless and warm, with the slow-moving water, and fishing nets, and ancient sampans you see in children's books like *The Story of Ping*—all of which it really did still have when we first visited in 1979. You may imagine my shock and dismay, therefore, when it suddenly showed up for the first time in my present world in a 2007 *New York Times* article about pollution: someone had written about the lake because it had started to luminesce.

An old picture of Lake Tai

The Yíxīng of a generation ago, in contrast, was a veritable Shangri-la, home to ancient forests of giant bamboo and a famous brownish-purplish clay that gets made into bonsai planters and world-class teapots. That clay is famous, not because it does not absorb odors, the distinction of so much Western cookware, but rather because it will absorb the flavor of every pot of tea made in it; so that over time, the many pots of the past come to lend an inimitable depth to what is steeped in it today. This idea

An Yíxīng teapot

of a prized quality that can only be achieved by slow accumulation over time is, by the way, characteristically Chinese, as is the interdependent suggestion that while the individual pot of tea is less than a be-all and end-all, it gains complexity and subtlety from the pots that preceded it and enriches the pots that follow.

In describing his grandfather, for example, my father first puts him, like a pot of tea, in generational

My father's grandfather

context: the youngest of a family of five boys, he is also the father of seven sons and six daughters by his wife, and an eighth son by a servant. Next comes his place in society. "He was a successful business-man," my father writes.

> He built 7 pawn shops in 7 villages around Yi-xing. That time, pawn shop[s] worked as small bank[s might] to-day. He also had 2 grocery stores [in 2 nearby vil-lages] which supplied all kinds of basics, such as rice, salt, cooking oil etc.[6]

Then, instead of describing his grandfather's appearance or personality or tastes—the sorts of things we in the West might include as a way of conveying both his uniqueness and his importance as a figure in the narrative—my father describes, at striking length and in striking detail, his context—namely, the family house.

This house, I will say, really was quite something. Even today my father will laugh to recall his advisor's shock when, as a doctoral student at the University of Minnesota many years later, he was asked how big his family's house was, and answered, "oh 400 rooms, something like that." When the house was torn down by the Communists, they made a movie of the demolition, that they might show it as a lesson to others; and in his autobiography, my father calls it simply "the biggest and best house in the town." It was, he writes,

> enclosed inside of a[n] 8 foot [high] white wall, the front [of which had] a set of 8 doors on South Main Street. Once [in] a while, one of these door[s would be] open. As you walk thru the door [there] was an open court yard and two rooms [,] one [to] each side. The right side room ha[d] another door to South Main Street which was open all the time. Then a hall, [which] open[ed to]

the courtyard. The back side of the hall [also had] two doors. On . . . [those] doors [were] posted [the] 8 words [that were] . . . the middle names for our 8 generations. These two doors [were] also closed most of the time.

And so on. The description continues for a number of paragraphs and includes two more sets of eight doors—eight, if you are wondering, being a lucky number because the word for "eight" in Chinese, *bā,* sounds like the word for "prosperity," *fā*—as well as numerous other spaces. For example,

My grand father's living quarter[s] . . . [were on the] other side of the long hall walk way. He has living room, two bedroom[s and] two studies, [and] one [of] his bedroom ha[d a] back bedroom [as well, that] connected [to] the 2nd garden. His second floor [was] just big as the first floor which we never was there.[7]

Is it a sign of Westernization that my father thinks to mention there being twenty or thirty servants as well, and how "Where they stay/sleep . . . i did not know"? Contrary, in any case, to what we Western readers might have learned to expect from narratives like *Heidi* and Harry Potter, he says nothing about where he slept, either.

Instead he seems to focus obsessively on the number of doors in the house, and whether they were open or shut. Over and over again we hear, "Once a while, one of these door was open . . . These two doors also closed most of the time . . . One end of the long hall walk way is the door in hall which we use the door all the time," and so on—passages in which we can still discern, I think, eighty years later, a little boy making his way through a highly socially constructed maze. Like the amount of room that his grandfather's suite takes up, which has clearly made an impression on him, the fact that access to certain spaces is being controlled—that certain doors are open and certain doors shut—has very much registered, too.

That power can literally open doors in this world is brought home by the most notable occasion of my father's early childhood, namely the marriage, when he was four years old, of his fifth aunt to the grandson of Féng Guózhāng, one of the "presidents" who came to power after the fall of the Qing Dynasty in 1911. Those of you who have visited or seen pictures of the Forbidden City in Beijing may recall the marble axis that runs down its middle, over which only the emperor was traditionally carried. Well, in conjunction with her wedding, my great-aunt was also carried over this axis. The enormous front gate of

The marble axis of the Forbidden City in Beijing

Close-up of the marble axis

the Forbidden City was opened for her as well; and so, perhaps somewhat less momentously and yet still momentously, were all three sets of eight doors in the Yíxīng family compound. As my father says,

> In my life time, I [only] saw all these doors open[ed] once[, for the] big wedding of my 5th aunt to the . . . [grand]son of Chinese President Fung. That day, we had two military bands [in the house,] one in each courtyard and [also] many high government officials.

All of which is to say that, before he describes any person, my father describes the power structure of his world as it was inscribed in its architecture.

In this, my father's account bears an intriguing resemblance to parts of *Six Records of a Life Adrift*, a rare and highly prized example of Chinese autobiography written in the nineteenth century by Shen Fu—a writer greatly esteemed in the East, though barely known in the West. This work was interestingly examined for its fitful plot by scholar Earl Miner, who offers as an example of its "essayistic" passages:

> Poor scholars who live in small crowded houses should rearrange their rooms in imitation of the sterns of the

Taiping boats of my home country, the steps of which can be made into three beds by extending them at the front and back. Each bed is then separated from its neighbor by a board covered with paper. Looking at them when they are laid out is like walking a long road —you do not have a confined feeling at all.

Is this narrative? Miner wants to know. An interesting question, though what we might recognize in this touching passage is perhaps a narrator not unlike my father, negotiating the givens of his world in a spirited and creative way. Shen Fu, too, seems less interested in describing himself than in describing his context, although—again like my father—he in fact conveys much about himself all the same. As Graham Sanders, a recent translator of the *Records,* compassionately notes, Shen Fu

continually constructs or encounters small, limited spaces—both physical and in his imagination—where he can feel and express his emotions [but is] constantly subjected to the pain of losing his small worlds.[8]

And so it is, perhaps, ultimately, with my father. He does find, in the world of opening and closing doors, places where we might imagine that he also escapes "a confined feeling." There is the front garden, with its cow and its vegetable and flower beds, and the back garden, with its pond and three small bridges. He recalls with obvious fondness the "Good size fishes . . . [that] swim on top of the water in the early morning[,] which I enjoyed very much," adding,

> [T]hose fish was rather big, 10–15 inches long in black or golden colors . . . I [would get] up in the morning, stay under the shade for few hours, just [to] watch those fishes.

As an aside, I might add here that there is a quality to this leisure that would stay with my father all his life—that to this day, he can sit outside and watch nothing much for hours on end, perfectly content. This is the part of him that liked to talk, in a Daoist way, about becoming a monk in the mountains,[9] and a part of him that resurfaces in his personal history when he talks about the "2 or 3 horses in town," and how "I also stay there to watch for 1 or 2 hours." It is there as well as when he describes his family's summer garden, which he says "was similar to the Back Garden but much bigger." My father remembers:

> Almost next [to] our summer Garden, there is a bridge over a small river. [If y]ou look at the water from the bridge [you will see] the water turn around and make . . . two swirls.

But, alas, what befalls Shen Fu befalls him; these things are lost to him for many, many years. We can only imagine what he feels when he writes,

> On my 60 year old birthday, I saw the swirls in the river again.

No love of swirls for his grandfather, in the meanwhile, whom my father continues to describe in terms of his social role:

> My grand father was well known as the richman in town. Also he was very generous and gave food, clothing, [and] medicines [to people], [as well as] helping [with] tuitions, paving city streets and [doing] many other . . . [things] for [them.]

He further notes that his grandfather

> also owned real estate in Shanghai [including] Several store building[s] on Nanking Road, which [was] equivalent to Fifth Ave of New York City

and so on. My father does mention, interestingly, that "Grand father always ha[d] 3 meal by himself"— even, it seems, during holidays—but does not speculate as to what this unusual practice might say about his grandfather's thoughts or feelings. Instead he focuses on the daily ritual involved—how someone would consult with the cook to decide each day's menu, and how "Each of the daughter[s]-in-law [would] take . . . [a] turn of 5 days" serving him. This is not a modern, linear world of conflict and rising action, but rather one of harmony and eternal, cyclical action, in which order, ritual, and peace are beauty, and events spell, not excitement or progress, but disruption. Writes my father,

> His children, grandchildren [and] daughter-in-laws must see him and [say] good mor[n]ing and good night to him. The same to Grand Mother.

And similarly,

> On the new years day, grand father and grand mother sat in two chairs [in the] middle of the formal reception hall with red carpet. My uncles lined up and kneel down, say happy new year to grand parents, next . . . [come] all grand sons, all daughter-in-laws, then all grand daughters. men are ahead of women.

So ingrained was the "men ahead of women" part of this, that even in 2007, when I went to Yíxīng to help with the reinterment of my grandmother's ashes, I was held back by a cousin, lest I board the minivan before the males in the family. In the photo I am paying respects when my turn in the lineup of women comes around.

Me paying respects to my grandmother

Reading between the lines, we can perhaps surmise that my father's grandmother lived to 103 despite having borne thirteen children in an era before antibiotics by sheer force of personality. My father tells us,

> Grand mother . . . run the house ho[l]d day-to-day business. She got up very early in the morning and order every body to work.

Also, on New Year's eve,

> after . . . dinner, grand mother wiped every body's mouth with . . . toilet tissue and kitchen God forgive us if we said some thing wrong during the year.

But the fullest portrait we get of anyone in these pages is of my father's mother: a healthy, open-minded woman named Hsu Pao-zao, who was born in 1890.[10] As for the source of her open-mindedness,

My father's mother with my father
and his number three brother

my father mostly attributes it, in interdependent style, not to something special about her, but to her family's factory in Shanghai. Because this factory made thermoses and candy tins, the "machineries and metal" for which were imported, and because they also exported their products, her family "was more exposed to [the] outside world than my family," my father says, and "regularly [had] contact with foreigners." We might note, though, that quite apart from this influence she was also apparently an intelligent woman, who "never went to school for formal education, but she learn to read by herself," and who realized, what's more, that "the world is different [now] . . . and we have to change our old way of Yi-xing thinking." She accomplished this in three ways. "First," my father says, she

> change clothing into American/British style[. T]he sec-
> ond change [was to] give my brother[s] a lot of freedom
> to develop themselves[.] The third [change] was [to]
> provide . . . money to them. The money was from our
> grand father.

Touchingly, he adds here, in one of his few digressions,

> She gave her life to serve [the] Jen family and gave her
> love to her own 5 sons. The only hope in her mind was

[that] some day her sons [would be] healthy and well. She had all kinds of Chinese old qualities and she gave the [most] important thing to us—lots of her love.

My mother was really great mother.

As for how this great mother came to be the modernizer of the family, that was thanks to her husband, my father's father, contracting syphilis in his early thirties. Though the family hung a sword over his bed that I was once told had belonged to Genghis Khan, it failed to scare away the evil spirits. He died

My father's father

instead, leaving my father's mother with five boys, including my father, the second to the youngest, who was four at the time. "To-day I still do not have any impression about my father," he heartbreakingly writes; and, indeed, aside from his memories of his mother, he has strikingly few memories of his childhood at all—something we will discuss in the next lecture. Certainly, he recounts few here, although he has recalled in person his brother breaking a plate on a holiday—a time when it was bad luck to do so—and accordingly being scolded, only to have his grandmother supply a whole stack of old dishes to throw against the wall. I have always imagined this scene as formative for my father, and see him, a young boy, watching his brother hurl and smash the plates in a way quite at odds with the American stereotype of the Chinese as shy and restrained: the idea was that a Jen boy was not supposed to feel inhibited in any way. You may imagine how it is that the first time I read *King Lear,* I thought, *That's my father.*

Though would Lear have described himself, as does my father, when he finally gets to himself on page eight, as "a happy country boy?" My father not having said anything more, you will have to accept my description of him as earthy, fun-loving, risk-taking, and mercurial—a man whose uniqueness may not have been much celebrated by his culture but who was nonetheless quite an original—begging the question whether individualism produces uniqueness or merely individuals who cherish and cultivate their uniqueness.

But never mind. The first real event of this narrative comes when my father is ten, and it is, sure enough, bad news.[11] He writes,

> That time Yi-xing regularly has riots. These rio[t]s are small group[s] of local people from mountains, they rob stores and kidnap children . . . [When I was] About . . . 10 years old, the riots were different. They had red handkerchief around their neck and hold long gun. Three of them came into our living room. My mother held my hand . . . [and] walk[ed] by them, It was lucky they did not stop us. We quickly walk[ed] into our hi[d]ing place which was built for emergency. [Our w]hole family hi[d] there for 3 days. The . . . [rioters] broke . . . many fine furniture . . . and opened many suitcases.

These were the Communists. My father finishes, "Lucky no body was hurt/killed," but he also describes the sudden flight of his grandfather: "Almost immediately after the riot, grandfather left Yi-xing [for] Shanghai." His grandfather had, in fact, frequently gone to Shanghai in the past, typically hiring an entire car of the train for the trip, and often taking my father's two oldest brothers with him, so as to expose them to the world. They would eat with forks and knives in Western restaurants, for example, toting along a thermos of warm Chinese wine with which to wash the strange food down. But this time my father's grandfather "distributed his money in[to] . . . 8 equal parts, [giving] 7 to his 7 sons and 1 to his first grandson." He was leaving for good.

When people talk about the traditional groupishness of the Chinese—about their propensity for living behind walls, and their reliance on systems of personal trust, rather than on a broader, more abstract, social trust—I often think of the bandits that plagued Yíxīng. Also I think of the general danger felt by many Asians, I think, to lurk right outside or even inside their door. Author Amy Chua, for example, recollects growing up in a Filipino Chinese diaspora community so rich and resented that her aunt was killed by her chauffeur in her own living room. "I'll never forget the police report," writes Chua. "At the line for 'motive' . . . [the chauffeur] had written just one word: revenge." And of course, it isn't only the rich diaspora Chinese who feel this insecurity. If anything, the lower classes feel it more, for a host

of reasons beginning with the long history of fam-
ine and flooding; the eternal shortage of arable
land; and the incessant political instability that in
the twentieth century alone included the fall of Imperial China, the Communist Revolution, the Cultural Revolution, the coming of State Capitalism,
and more. What surprise can it be, really, that the
Chinese tend to circle the wagons, or that this overwhelming fundamental insecurity surfaces in the
narratives they tell?

We see this in older European narratives and in
those of other Asians, too. Writer Andrew Lam, for
example, observes that "despite the age of high-tech
wizardry, [contemporary Japanese] manga/anime
continues to distill an ancient ethos of the Far East,"
noting that

> if American fairy tales are in the business of protect-
> ing children from the reality of a cold and belligerent
> world, Japanese fairy tales told through certain genre
> of mangas and animes are doing quite the opposite:
> preparing their charges for the day in which their nor-
> mal and seemingly sunny life may be abruptly thrown
> into complete chaos and destruction.

What's more, my father's narrative interestingly
calls to mind African American narratives as well,
which, psychologist Dan McAdams has pointed out,

often follow a mainstream American narrative focused on chosenness, pilgrimage, and redemption, but with two differences. I'll come to the second of these in a minute.

The first, meanwhile, is an emphasis on early danger: instead of a "once upon a time," fairytale-like opening to their stories, there is often danger from the get-go—Frederick Douglass being taken from his mother as an infant, for example—African American autobiographies generally highlighting, as McAdams notes, "the need to be vigilant in a world that can never be fully trusted." Now, we've seen, of course, that my father does paint his earliest years with the brush of nostalgia. But as with African American narratives, the very first event my father relates—namely, the coming of the Communists, the hiding in the garden, and the departure of his grandfather—bespeaks danger. What's more, the event that follows right on its heels does, too.

This event is connected to a dream in which, my father says, his grandfather saw

> a dying big tree, but [with] one branch vigorously [coming] out. He thought the branch was my mother's children.

It was a dream that had implications for my father because his grandfather's oldest brother had no children, and the plan, therefore, had been for him to adopt my father. My father would have inherited a sizable amount of money in this way; and given how many grandsons there were, it must have seemed a reasonable arrangement. Still, as a result of the dream, his grandfather, writes my father,

> ask[ed] my mother and I [to] go to Shanghai to see him. After he saw me . . . he changed his mind [and decided] not [to] give me away to [his] brother, but [instead to keep] me as his grand son.

Was my father too integral a twig of the vigorous branch to give away? Did his grandfather see something in him that day—maybe what my father himself would later call his "drive"? And did that drive have its source in some combination of a fear that he—a boy who had already lost his father to syphilis—could be given away, and a desire to prove his grandfather right in declining to do so? In any case, it's one of the few stories my father tells about his life, and one, I think, that has meant more to him than anything; and though the danger he faced was in no way as overwhelming as Douglass's, his reprieve is similarly tied up with a sense of chosenness.

The second difference between mainstream

American and African American narratives noted by McAdams is that African American narratives commonly feature "an opponent with whom the protagonist does battle." This opponent is typically something external, such as "the street," and the struggles against this are frequently cast as between good and evil, with the protagonist of the tale enjoined, above all, to keep to a straight and narrow path. He quotes, for example, one "highly generative Black woman" as saying,

> "I'm always preaching to my kids, you know, you can make it, but you can't detour, you have to just keep a straight and narrow path toward the goal"... Unswerving focus on goals is the key to success, suggested another: "So most of what I can remember really, growing up is the schooling, the discipline you got, you know, like marching really, strictly toward goals." In stories like these, losing sight of one's goals almost invariably leads to trouble.

And so it might, my father seems to feel, for him, too. His early education is continually disrupted and of poor quality. As he writes wryly,

> Because [of] the riots in the town we did not go to the elementary school, but have a teacher at home ...
> The teacher have lunch with us. He watched our ta-

ble manners . . . by the time [I was] 11 years old, I was still in 5th grade.

The shame of this is brought home when, thanks to the Japanese occupation of Shanghai, some cousins come to live with them. "One of them was a year younger [than I, but] he [had already] entered [the] first year of a jr high," says my father, recalling, "I felt bad." He subsequently tries to catch up.

> My second brother suggested I skip one year [and try to go straight into the] Jr high, [so I took] the entrance examination . . . Unfortunately, I did not pass and failed. I felt very bad and cried. My second brother [then] suggested [I] take the entrance examination again. I passed the second time.

Notable here is the sudden appearance of exams as critical gates—doors—to achievement. He goes on,

> In the two years at the Jr high, I was doing fairly good, but not that great. My second brother suggested that I skip again [straight] in to high school in Shanghai. He put me into the high school [of] which he was the vice principal. My third brother was the treasur[er].

I should say here that it was not uncommon in China at that time for people to buy schools and run them as businesses, and I'm sure many little

brothers got enrolled in them as well. Lest we somehow harbor the fantasy that all Chinese education
was of stellar quality and that all Chinese students
studied hard, that's to say, we might note my father's descriptions of his brothers' school and the
hints of "the street" in it:

> That high school was a play school, no body was really
> interested in study, but dance and parties . . .
>
> Dance—Only [a] few days after [we] enter[ed] the
> school, some [dancers] came and offered dance lessons
> for free. [D]id not take long, my classmate[s] went to
> dance and go[t] in to a[ll] kinds of trouble . . . , such as
> sex with these dancing girls.
>
> Great World Play Ground—Operated by mafia, all
> kinds [of] trouble[. . .], such as gambling etc
>
> The 4th avenue—[A] Hundred prostitutes lined up
> on the street.

He soon transferred to another school.

> This high [school] was well known as very rough [and]
> also operated by mafia.
>
> The school required [a] short hair cut and [a] school
> uniform which is rather unusual in Shanghai. The first
> day, all [the] students lined up and waited for the prin-
> cipal. After [a] very long wait . . . , [finally] the principal
> showed up. He start[ed off by] say[ing,] . . . You know I
> killed 600 communists before, you better behave nicely.

As a result, "It was true in the class room, no such thing as wise guy," my father observes, but concludes, "I just do not like the atmosphere." And so it was on to yet another school that, he says, "was not serious about books, but sports."

So far he has yet to find the straight and narrow path to which he must keep, but what have emerged are threats—the "street" and also an even greater enemy, indolence. Clearly related to his grandfather's dream that the other branches of the family were going to die is my father's observation that "In general 27th generation did not do too much. May be because their father has money, they do not have [to do] any thing for [a] living." Vis-à-vis his aunts, he reports, "All my aunts and my uncle[s'] wives did not say or do anything." And he relates with stark simplicity how

> During Japanese time, [Sixth Uncle] was in Chungqing. His wife always ill in bed. She does not do any thing in the house. One day [my] uncle made a pan cake with rats poison. Killed himself in Chungqing.

This suicide is not elaborated on in his memoir; neither has my father ever said much about it in person. All he ever said about his uncles was "Those guys working? Are you kidding?" and "No drive"—"no drive" being, in my father's book, one of the most damning criticisms that could be made of a person.

The opposite of this was a focused tenacity we associate even today with Asians and Asian Americans, and which my father began to exhibit when, while he was in the high school focused on sports, he met someone who would prove very important to him. He writes,

> My room mate, Mr Chen [who was] also from Yi-xing . . . was very serious and would like to enter a good national college. After 10 pm [when] the el[e]ctric light [was] turned off, he always . . . [lit] a candle light [so he could] continue study[ing] . . . After [we finished] high school, he asked me to study with him for [the] college entrance examination. I did. The result of this study put me into National Central University.

Much has been made of the centrality of Chinese civil service exams, which began in the Han Dynasty and became an all-consuming focus in the Song, dominating Chinese life for close to a thousand years afterward. These were the exams through which people qualified for government positions, and one of the major origins of the Asian emphasis on scholarship. Held at the local, provincial, and national level, they were the single greatest route to wealth and power available, and also the single greatest focus of any family that could afford to support a son in studies. Today many kids kill themselves trying to get into Harvard; you can imagine what the pressure would be if graduation qualified them for, say, a governorship. My mother's father, who passed the provincial level exam at a young age, was welcomed home by a band; and the Jens are still proud to recall not only that thirty-three family members passed the provincial level exam over the years, but that fourteen of them passed the national exam as well. Such is the importance of these scholar officials to the family that their names take pride of place in the updated family genealogical book, following right on the heels of the genealogical chart itself.

Of course, in the Republican era of my father's youth the exam system was officially defunct. Still, the failing and passing of exams remained very much part of the Chinese cultural template, as it still is: witness the all-important college-entrance *gāokǎo* in China today and, some would say, the preoccupation of some Asian Americans with standardized tests. Yours truly, I should say here, was not in this category, having neither done any special preparation for my SATs, way back when, nor signed my son up for any special tutoring or courses. But when I read about how the entering class of an elite exam school like Stuyvesant High School in New York is, as it will be in September, a whopping 72 percent Asian American, I think of the tremendous focus on my older brother's performance when we were growing up, and of my father's recollections of exams that were graded to the hundredth of a point. It is no exaggeration when my father describes his passing of the university exam as "big news." He recalls,

the names who passed the examination of National Central University w[ere] published in [the] News paper. Of course, my second brother and 2nd sister-in-law were very proud of me.[12]

Sadly, the Mr. Chen who had studied with my father did not pass. And this, too, is where my father's story and African American narratives diverge—what with the millennia of cultural support in China for people with this particular sort of "drive,"[13] and its support, too, of this sort of attainment. To the picture of lifelong vigilance, that's to say, is added, not only the idea that one must stick to a straight and narrow path, but a real straight and narrow path that leads predictably to stability and success. Many in academia have observed that the nature of this path is and isn't compatible with American educational ideals: I am struck every year by how consistently President Drew Faust's addresses to Harvard freshmen emphasize free exploration and playfulness—an emphasis appropriate to a stable, egalitarian, individualistic society. And one can easily see that while the Chinese template can be readily adapted to tracks such as that for engineering or medicine, it is wildly at odds with Western ideas about art, as we will be discussing in the next lecture. It is, rather, far closer to the kind of piano "training" described in Amy Chua's *Battle Hymn of the Tiger Mother*—a book to which most of my friends reacted with horror but which, I have been told, at least one African American law professor handed out as a kind of blueprint to his children.

The traditional Chinese template, that's to say, was geared toward attaining safety and social standing in a dangerous, interdependent, hierarchical world, with a clear center of which my father was aware from a very young age. If we return to the picture we imagined earlier of my father growing up, watching fish, in other words, we must add to it now one of the glass-bottomed pavilions his family had—one in the back garden of their main house and one in their summer garden—for it is in one of these that he is lying on his stomach, face pressed to the glass, watching. The water is green. The air is very still—like the air inside of a balloon, protected from normal currents. It is hot. And yet for all that, even as a young boy my father is aware that the glass inset and its underlying rock grotto are a special thing, a thing no one else in the province has; and though perhaps he would have liked watching fish in any case, an inextricable part of his pleasure is knowing that the pavilion is modeled on one in an imperial garden in Beijing—a pavilion my father's grandfather saw when attending the big wedding that opened all the doors.

That wedding was later seen as a source of bad luck: people said that as punishment for the hubris of having been carried up the central axis of the Forbidden City, my father's aunt never had any children. But be that as it may, the Beijing wedding left a deep impression on her father, my father's grandfather, who upon his return modeled many features of his own summer garden on what he'd seen—not only the pavilion, but the windows in the arcade leading to it, for example, and the distinctive green tile work by which, when my family went back in 1979, my father recognized the hotel at which we were staying to be, in fact, located on what had been his family's property. That is to say that the hierarchical framework was everywhere, even outside, even in my father's moments of apparent freedom. We can only imagine what Michel Foucault would

My father revisiting the old Jen family summer garden

think of a center of power this omnipresent and a kind of Appian Way to get there; it is a long way from Walden Pond.

And yet it produced then, as it can today, educational results we respect. My father talks about how only a few days after he began his college studies, the "Japanese airplane dropped bombs in Nanking and in National Central University," as a result of which the university had to move inland. We can fill in the picture readily enough—the suspension of classes, the posting of notices, the packing of boxes and writing of letters. My father, though, gives us none of this. Instead, with Confucian-style didacticism, he pauses after explaining the situation to note what he clearly feels is most important, namely his admiration for the president of the university, who "made quick decision to move the University to Chungqing." He writes,

> I very much respect his decision as his biggest contribution to our University, He ha[d] foresight and saw what will happen in the years ahead.[14] This move made the University . . . the best University in China.

Only after having discharged this observation does he really turn to the action, explaining how they had to move the entire school, by boat, upstream, up the

Yangtze River. This had some movie-worthy moments—for example, in the gorges when "The boat does not have enough power to move forward," and the captain had to order many books be thrown overboard. This was followed by equipment. "Then [he] got a group of people 20–30 pull a rope, [and] the boat moved up a few miles," my father writes.

As for life in mountainous Chongqing, in the interior, when they finally reached it: there were friendly people, much beauty, and cheap prices, especially for oranges, but there was also sand in the rice, which my father says, "gave me stomach bleeding ulcer." It was just lucky that there were other family members in the city, including my father's number two brother, who gave my father his only mosquito net—a favor, my father says, "which I shall always remember of him." Harder to foil than the mosquitoes, though, were the "Japanese airplanes with bombs and machine guns," which, after all the trauma of the move, the school now faced again.

Thank goodness the mountains had many natural caves that could serve as bomb shelters. "Each cave can take 100 persons or more," my father says, recalling how once he was in one when it was bombed:

One day we were inside one of these caves [when a] Japanese airplane dropped a bomb on top of the hill. The mud and rock slid . . . down [closing] one [of] the entrance[s] next to cave and killed more than 100 persons inside . . . Few days after the bomb, My classmates did not see me and believed I was killed. Th[e]y prepared a funeral service for me. At that hour, I walked into the classroom.

Shades of Tom Sawyer and Huck Finn. In sum, "We had very rough environmental living conditions," says my father. "However, our Professors still gave best lectures and we learn just [as] much as if the disturbances were not there."

Just like American students! He goes on, "[Our] professors said: these students do not need professors to teach them. They only need a [text] book." Of course, the professors did hold class anyway, enabling my father to conclude that, the difficulties notwithstanding, "the experience in the University [was] . . . the most valuable experience . . . in my life."

There is more to my father's story. Among other things, he went on to become a professor himself here in America, and to work on the atomic bomb program called "Starfish." And let me point out that his overall narrative is nowhere near so linear as it would appear by my stopping here. But, well, there it is. There is much talk these days about the Chinese and creativity; for what it's worth, my father went on to be a person who thought to work on turbulent plasma when everyone else was working on steady state plasma, and to prove strikingly—my mother would probably say maddeningly—unconventional. I might mention here, also, that writer Malcolm Gladwell's observation about the level of mastery needed to generate innovation in a given field—that it involves at least 10,000 hours—puts traditional Chinese focus in an interesting light.

My father retired many decades ago, but he still

My father lecturing at the City College of New York

has the plaque that sat on his desk that reads "Professor Norman Jen." We'll be talking about his teaching methods in the third lecture. First, though, we will have a look at some studies that put both my father's story and, when we get to it, my own, in revealing perspective.

2

ART, CULTURE, AND SELF

In the first lecture we talked about my father, and his narrative about growing up in Yíxīng. We saw how little he focused on interior states or on the distinguishing characteristics that mark a person as unique but rather described his grandfather, for example, in terms of his role and place in society. We saw, too, how much more emphasis in general my father placed on his context than on what we in the West might think the proper focus of an autobiography, namely himself. And in these things, he gave us a sense of how at least one interdependent self told his life's story, even as he furnished a kind of chapter in that intellectual autobiography I promised John Stauffer—the "roots" chapter.

This lecture will have two distinct parts. The first

will involve doing something I've never done before, namely give a little science talk. I do this not because I have always wanted to be a cognitive psychologist, but because the recent research on inter-/independence and narrative sheds a most interesting light on both my father's narrative and, as we will see, narrative in general. Then, in the second half, we will move to the novel and how all we have been discussing about culture, small c, feeds into Culture, capital C, and vice versa. That is to say that, armed with our inter-/independence lens, we will be looking at some pictures and texts as a way of grasping, among other things, just how individualistic Western art and narrative are—a subject that will enable me to begin to relate how I, a daughter raised in a distinctly interdependent way, came to do a distinctly independent thing.

But first: on with my science hat, and off to the work of a number of cross-cultural psychologists, but especially that of Cornell psychologist Qi Wang. She is hardly the only researcher to have looked at the difference in self-construction we will be discussing. Quite the contrary, there have been any number of psychologists working in this field, including Hazel Markus and Shinobu Kitayama, who introduced the terms "independent" and "interdependent" in 1991. However, Qi Wang's work has been of particularly galvanizing interest to me because of her cutting-edge work on self-construction and narrative.

She does not directly address the novel. However, in a series of experiments begun in the late 1980s, she found that Asians, Asian-born immigrants, and even the children of those immigrants—second-generation Americans like me—tend to tell very different self-narratives than European Americans; and that this difference is linked to deeper differences in self-construction. That is to say that Wang and her colleagues have found that while contemporary European Americans, brought up to treasure their uniqueness as individuals, tend to tell long narratives about themselves that help illuminate, explain, and celebrate what is special about them, Asians and Asian Americans typically do not.

Of course, there are exceptions among both Easterners and Westerners—differences between populations are often belied by what we see in individuals. What's more, a Vietnamese is not a Korean, recent immigrants are not older immigrants, a Hong Kong Chinese is not an Yíxīng Chinese, and the children of a Pakistani professor may be a far cry from their cousins, let alone the children of a Japanese profes-

sor. Still, if we were to plot Westerners versus Easterners with regard to relative inter- or independence,
we would get two distinct curves, with a significant
area of overlap, but significant displacement between them, too. As University of Michigan psychologist Richard Nisbett puts it, "Variations between
and within societies, as well as within individuals,
should not blind us to the fact that there are very
real differences, substantial on the average, between
East Asians and people of European culture." Such
is the difference in degree of self-focus, in fact, that
it is, in Nisbett's words, as if "Westerners are protagonists of their autobiographical novels; [and]
Asians . . . merely cast members in movies touching
on their existences."

This perhaps portrays the interdependent self
as more passive than it is. Though, as we saw in the
last lecture, the collectivist self can be more accept-
ing of certain realities than the independent or individualistic self, acceptance hardly constitutes passivity. Quite the contrary, it can, in fact, engender
the opposite—not a confrontational self, necessarily,
or at least not one that confronts its own group[1]—
but a fiercely enterprising, unselfconscious, navigatory self. (Think rollerbladers and an obstacle
course, and you'll have the idea.) What's more,

the independent self can be a navel-gazer extraordinaire.

Still, if we think back to other aspects of my father's narrative, we may appreciate Nisbett's point: my father's role in his narrative about his childhood could hardly be called that of a protagonist. Witness, too, an experiment Wang published in 2009, in which Asian-born and European American Cornell undergraduates were asked to keep a journal for a week.[2] At the end of the week they were given a pop quiz, with results that were, I think, astonishing: for never mind the much-remarked-upon prowess of Asian Americans at test-taking, when tested on the events of their own lives, these subjects scored at the bottom of the class. So other-focused were they that, in contrast to their more self-focused European American classmates, they struggled to remember their own entries in their own journals.[3] Similarly, in a related study, the recollections of Asian American adults were shown to focus far more on group actions and interpersonal relations than on their own experiences, as well as to envision social situations from the perspective of others rather than from their own.

Of course, in this they displayed a most useful skill for fiction writing: an editor at Houghton Mifflin once told me that in trying to assess the potential of a young writer, he liked to look at the quality of the secondary characters—gauging in this way the author's awareness of others besides him or herself. But the other-centeredness of the Asian and Asian American subjects of Qi Wang's experiments will also remind us, perhaps, of W. E. B. Du Bois's observations regarding African American double-consciousness: "this sense," as he said, "of always looking at one-self through the eyes of others, of measuring one's soul by the tape of a world that looks on in amused contempt and pity." The typical focus of envisioning in the case of Asians and Asian Americans is not the self; nor is it infused with contempt and pity. But neither is it the "natural" self-focus of many European Americans—as I probably could have told you, I should say here, and as my longtime editor at Knopf, Ann Close, probably could have as well. Hattie Kong, the protagonist of my most recent novel, *World and Town,* for example, was originally a set of eyes and ears, with no real story of her own; and so she might have stayed, were it not for Ann's gracious nudging.

Let us not stray off into literature quite yet, though, but rather stay for now with how the success of that nudging interestingly corroborates the results of another of Qi Wang's studies, in which she describes how Asian Americans can be "primed" in such a way as to tap into either their more Western or more Asian self. Of course, in showing sensitivity to priming, Asian Americans are no different than anyone else, Western or Eastern; all people can be primed. In this particular study, however, when Asian Americans were first asked a series of questions in an independent vein—to describe themselves as unique individuals, for example, or to circle the word "I" in a number of sentences—they were subsequently found "more likely to recall more memories of exclusive personal interest and [to] focus . . . on their own roles and perspectives" than if primed with questions of an interdependent bent. The underlying memories here were not, as Wang put it, "overwhelmed"; they did not simply morph into something else altogether. They were, however, filtered differently and thereby subtly altered. (As all memories are wont to be, we may recall. Remember, for instance, how that Native American ghost tale Frederic Bartlett used in the memory experiment we talked about in the first lecture changed each time it was recollected by its British recounters.)

But be that as it may, Qi Wang's very striking, more general, and more literarily germane finding is that, brought up to define ourselves in relationship to others, many Asians and Asian Americans not only tend to recall fewer life events than European Americans but also tend to tell—and record—fewer, shorter, less elaborate self-narratives. There have been exceptions, beginning with Shen Fu's *Six Records of a Life Adrift,* which we talked about in the first lecture. For the scholars among you, the quasi-autobiographical Japanese "I novels" (the *Watakushi shosetsu*) might also come to mind, or *Biographical Literature (Zhuanji Wenxue),* a popular contemporary Taiwanese journal whose pages often feature or draw upon memoir. But the volume of Asian autobiographical writings is still a trickle compared to that of the West; and the tenor of self-narratives with Asian roots is also often gentler and lower key, focusing on the typical and harmonious and including more general memories of the "in the summer we slept in the day and did things at night" type.[4] European American self-narratives, in contrast, tend to be more linear, featuring specific, dramatic, one-time events of the "so I let him have it" variety.

What's more, Wang fascinatingly shows this difference in narrative thrust to stem not from, say, differences in ideas about what makes a good story, but from differences in what is perceived and encoded by the brain—these last two things being intimately linked to each other as well as to what cognitive psychologists call "episodic memory." Unlike "semantic memory," which is a kind of storage bank for general knowledge and facts, "episodic memory" is the storage bank for personal events. And, as the memory for things that take place in time, it is both highly associated with the sort of self-narration we've been discussing, and on average less keenly developed in Eastern populations than Western.

Not, please note, that the Eastern brain is somehow less developed overall. Reflecting its culture, though, it has developed in response to its own priorities, which is to say that the same way a poet's biceps may reflect more interest in meter-making than in muscle-making, the interdependent episodic memory has a capacity reflective of interdependent values. Of course, just as a poet might well come to write many more poems than he or she might have otherwise thanks to the state of his or her biceps, the interdependent self might well come to recall an ever smaller number of events, thanks to its relatively weak episodic memory, and focus ever more holistically instead. And this in turn might render it ever more interdependent in outlook and ever less demanding of its episodic memory, which is then ever less stimulated to develop, etcetera—even as the independent self, in its own feedback loop, recalls an ever larger number of events, rendering it ever more independent in outlook and ever more demanding of its episodic memory, and so on. Our brains are at once miraculously plastic and ruinously rut-prone.

All of which is to say that the interesting answer to the question posed by the title of Qi Wang's journal-keeping study—"Are Asians Forgetful?"—is no. Asians are not forgetful; personal events are not forgotten. Rather, they are never mentally filed away to begin with because they are filtered out before they can be. That is to say that even if directed, as these Cornell Asian-born students were, to record their week's events in their journals, the events are not retained by their episodic memories because the students do not perceive them as salient. Instead, the same cultural filtering that we spoke of as having affected memory retrieval in both Wang's "priming" experiment and Frederic Bartlett's narrative recall experiment in this case helps select what is perceived and encoded from the outset.

What's more, the filtering turns out to apply not only to autobiographical memories and matters pertaining to the self, but to other matters as well. That is to say that the perceptual difference we have thought of up to now as a matter of simple self- or other-centeredness is actually far more than that. In fact, in keeping with a cultural emphasis on the interdependence of both people and things, the Asian-born students in this same journal-keeping study were found to parse their perceptions into larger chunks than did their European American classmates, regardless of subject matter—focusing on groups and relationships instead of items and distinctions, and weaving things together more than they teased them apart. Even when reading a narrative with no particular bearing on them, they parsed texts into fewer "events" than did their European American peers, as we can see in the text examples on the next page. The European American readers parsed the passage in question into seven segments, as shown in the top text, conceiving lines like "Came back upstairs and took a shower which is a confusing experience here" as containing two separate events, coming back and taking a shower. In contrast, the Asian-born readers conceived of that same line as a single event, and accordingly, as you can see in the text on the bottom, ended up parsing the passage as a whole into four segments. This is related to something I myself did, by the way, in the last lecture—presenting "the coming of the Communists, the hiding in the garden, and the departure of my father's grandfather" as a single event

... ⊥March 6th. A long talk with my brother Pete over breakfast this morning about family history and our parents' elopement and marriage —— all of these things fascinating to us and not so to our spouses and deadly boring to our children, and that's why you hang out with your siblings. ⊥Came back upstairs and ⊥took a shower which is a confusing experience here. One should not be irked by such a small thing, one should focus on larger spiritual things, but English plumbing is in its early experimental stage, I believe. Lots of pipes and tubes and faucets and gizmos, but you get the water going out of the shower head and the temperature keeps changing. And tiny adjustments of the faucets produce vast temperature swings. A man hates to spend 15 min taking a shower, for crying out loud. ⊥My niece Becky came over, who lives an hour from London and owns a glassware shop. It's odd to be related to somebody with that accent, who refers to motorways lifts and pronounces bath bawth. But then she comes from the southern branch of the family that fled the winter and took off for Florida forty years ago. They have their own odd accents and they're all Baptists. ⊥Pete and I went to a play "The Wonderland" in the afternoon, ⊥and then had supper with the British wing of the family tonight. (At an Italian restaurant.) ⊥Except Pete was going to a football game. He is, for reasons none of us can understand, a passionate soccer fan and is going to take the Tube out to a distant suburb and sit quietly in the stands among drunken burly obscene men. ⊥March 7th....

... ⊥March 6th. A long talk with my brother Pete over breakfast this morning about family history and our parents' elopement and marriage – all of these things fascinating to us and not so to our spouses and deadly boring to our children, and that's why you hang out with your siblings. ⊥Came back upstairs and took a shower which is a confusing experience here. One should not be irked by such a small thing, one should focus on larger spiritual things, but English plumbing is in its early experimental stage, I believe. Lots of pipes and tubes and faucets and gizmos, but you get the water going out of the shower head and the temperature keeps changing. And tiny adjustments of the faucets produce vast temperature swings. A man hates to spend 15 min taking a shower, for crying out loud. ⊥My niece Becky came over, who lives an hour from London and owns a glassware shop. It's odd to be related to somebody with that accent, who refers to motorways lifts and pronounces bath bawth. But then she comes from the southern branch of the family that fled the winter and took off for Florida forty years ago. They have their own odd accents and they're all Baptists. ⊥Pete and I went to a play "The Wonderland" in the afternoon, and then had supper with the British wing of the family tonight. (At an Italian restaurant.) Except Pete was going to a football game. He is, for reasons none of us can understand, a passionate soccer fan and is going to take the Tube out to a distant suburb and sit quietly in the stands among drunken burly obscene men. ⊥March 7th....

Above: reading passage from Qi Wang's study, "Are Asians Forgetful?" highlighted by a European American participant; *below*: the same passage highlighted by an Asian-born American participant

rather than as three separate events. As for whether, I, too, would therefore test the way the Asian-born students did on a recall test, I don't know; I did write the passage, after all. But in any case, what with their synthetic bent, this test group later recalled both fewer episodes and fewer details from their reading than did their more analytical European American peers.

Now, no one, to my knowledge, has run this experiment in reverse, to see if Asian and Asian American subjects recalled the big picture better than their European American peers or if they were quicker to grasp, say, a complex ecology or system. It would be interesting, though, to know what the results of such an experiment would be. In the meanwhile, Wang's research explains much about the broad focus and unelaborated texture of my father's narrative. What's more, it is in keeping with the many studies that show that given, say, a figure in a context, Asians tend to focus on the context, and Westerners, on the figure.[5] So pronounced can this perceptual predisposition be that in a 2007 study, some elderly Singaporean men were shown a series of pictures with a change of figure, as you can see in the right column of photographs in the next illustra-

Unchanging figure with changing background on the left and changing figure with unchanging background on the right

tion, from bucket to guitar to vacuum to plant—only to have their fMRIs show no indication whatsoever of brain activity.[6] They did, though, readily register a change when they were shown the pictures in the left column, a series in which the context of a bird was altered in ways that might seem subtle to Westerners. The Singaporeans did also, by the way, notice a change in the figure when explicitly instructed to pay attention to it. But their striking habit was to place their attention on what Westerners tend to think of as the background—the very word "background" suggesting how it is conceived.[7]

I would be remiss not to note here that these elderly Singaporeans represent an extreme case; even if it is not their focus, most Easterners do register the figure. However, they tend to see it holistically, as if the figure and context form a unit from which the figure is inextricable. Westerners, in contrast, tend to isolate the figure, perceiving it as wholly independent of, and eminently divorceable from, its surroundings—a difference that seems to me to inform our respective views of justice and responsibility, by the way, as well as our approaches to illness and medicine, and that may also have contributed to the long-held perception of Asians as possessing an ancient wisdom. Of course, there are many factors in a phenomenon like this last one; I do not mean to "explain" it per se. But thanks to the sort of perceptual differences we've been discussing, Westerners have tended over the millennia, as Nisbett and others have noted, to make discoveries involving discrete objects and to excel in logic and categorization. Easterners, meanwhile, have tended to think categorization simplistic and to be quicker to grasp holistic phenomena like acoustic resonance and magnetism, especially phenomena involving subtle, recurrent change, such as the relationship between the moon and the tides. It's not hard to imagine that these sorts of things might at one time have had, and indeed may still retain, a mystical feel for Westerners.

But on to the objections many of you must have. Can you really talk about East and West like that, to begin with, as if they are stable entities, and doesn't the very word "culture" conjure up islands, whereas we all know a culture to be more, as anthropologist Clifford Geertz put it, like an octopus, "a rather badly integrated creature" with "what passes for a brain [keeping] it together, more or less, in one ungainly whole"? And aren't there "many possible, ambiguous models of selfhood on offer even in simple or ritualized cultures," as psychologist Jerome

Bruner has said, and don't the psyche and culture, as anthropologist Richard Shweder put it, make each other up? And what about class—the suggestion some have made that interdependence and lower socioeconomic status are linked in any culture? Then there's social change—the dissolution, for example, first of the family and then of work units on a mainland China recently saturated to boot with ideas about individual enterprise and desire. My husband, reading this talk in draft, called this the CYA section of the hour—"CYA" being a business-world acronym for "cover your ass." He also pointed out that attempts to answer every possible objection to the studies we've talked about so far would mean no dinner for anyone, including him.

So let me just say that I have indeed, in the interests of time and dinner, presented a simplified picture. To cite only one of many studies that would bring this picture closer to reality, we might note that in places like, say, Beijing and Shanghai, some of the much-fussed-over "little emperors" who have resulted from the one-child rule have begun to show more developed autobiographical memories than the American children of Chinese immigrants—at least up until age three. Then, fascinatingly, this pattern was found to reverse: in a clear show of the power of environment, by the end of preschool, it was the Western-educated Asian American children who possessed the more developed episodic memories. What with mainland educators greatly concerned about the spoiling of the little emperors, there had apparently been so concerted an effort to get the kids "to observe rules and regulations, be polite to teachers, follow rules in games, and think about others" that the children involved did indeed come to more closely resemble other Chinese children.

And should any of you be wondering, despite Nisbett's comment about "the West and the rest," whether Asians are somehow genetically disposed toward an interdependent self, I'd like to point out a study conducted by psychologist Shinobu Kitayama and his colleagues on the Hokkaido Japanese. The Hokkaido Japanese, having voluntarily immigrated to the northernmost of the Japanese islands, mostly for economic reasons, have been shown to be highly individualistic[8]—almost as individualistic, in fact, as European Americans (who are, as it happens, the most independently oriented people in the world).[9] In this, they stand in dramatic contrast to the mainstream Japanese population from which they came —some combination of the experience of immigration and possibly the extreme weather having, it seems, made them that way.

Other observations of interest might include Richard Nisbett's remark that with regard to individualism "the Mediterranean countries plus Belgium and Germany are intermediate between the East Asian countries on the one hand and the countries most heavily influenced by Protestant, Anglo-Saxon culture on the other";[10] undoubtedly there is variation among the countries in which interdependence predominates as well. And undoubtedly, too, there is variation over time in every culture. For example, as John Demos noted in his Massey Lectures, *Circles and Lines,* for seventeenth-century American colonists, "self was decidedly *off* center." In the diaries of the nineteenth century, though, it becomes

> evident overall how much these people, these autobiographers, were writing for their own benefit," and "rather enjoyed the sound of their own voices (or at least the look of their own prose) . . . [their accounts, moreover, having] a very clear, sharp, indeed linear structure . . . from a beginning, through a middle . . . to an end.

Isn't this the very population that inspired Alexis de Tocqueville to coin the word "individualism"? In any case, it won't be long before a special synergy between American-ness and autobiography will be noted by many—with, for example, the subject of one of Thoreau's Concord Lyceum lectures recorded as "History of Himself," and the subject of the next, "Same as last week."[11]

For all of these and other possible refinements of the picture, though, the general truth still holds: there is a quickstep involving modernity, linearity, individualism, the isolated, the particular, and the extraordinary for which the hopskip of Western art, complete with its emphasis on art for art's sake and also on genius—on a conception of art as proceeding from a sacred spark within—is, as we will see, but a natural variation. And there is a quickstep, too, involving tradition, cyclicality, interdependence, the holistic, the general, and the quotidian, with which the hopskip of Eastern art, complete with its emphasis on moral utility, and also on mastery—on artistry as a thing tied to study and practice—twines equally naturally.

We will be coming to the art part of this talk soon—the Culture with a capital C section I've been promising. First, though, in the last segment of my little science unit, I'd like to talk about how inter- or independence of self is passed on—one large factor, unsurprisingly, being maternal style:[12] Qi Wang and other researchers have observed that Chinese mothers, and especially Chinese immigrant mothers, tend to use what researchers call a "low-elaborative" conversational style. That is to say that they engage in "short and directive conversations with their children . . . provide very little embellishment or detail . . . and often try to elicit correct answers."[13] It is a style that the children of these mothers will of course recognize, but that many who have had dealings with mainland Chinese education may well know, too. Writer Peter Hessler, for example, describes in *River Town* how little disposed at least one of his Chinese teachers was to encouraging comments, and how likely she was to pronounce something that was mostly right, plain wrong—*búduì!* And, in a related phenomenon, I recall how even in the highly progressive Beijing Montessori preschool to which I sent my daughter in 2003, the first Chinese phrase she learned was *Bié dòng!*—meaning, "Don't move!"

The emphasis of low-elaborative mothers and teachers, in short, is on proper behavior, self-restraint, and attunement to others. (I myself only wish I had a penny for every time I heard the phrase "consideration for others" growing up—though I should probably also note that, as my mother can attest, the low-elaborative approach has been known to backfire.)[14] High-elaborative mothers, meanwhile, "frequently . . . commented and expanded on memory responses . . . [and i]n doing so . . . scaffolded children's participation and . . . provided a narrative structure for the construction of elaborate personal stories." Of course, as the "little emperors" study we talked about a minute ago suggests, maternal shaping can be later modified by the larger culture.[15]

But whatever the means of imprint, children's narratives in particular often show a clear cultural mark. Witness, for example, the studies detailed in psychologist Allyssa McCabe's *Chameleon Readers,* in which McCabe and her colleagues fascinatingly show that Japanese kids tend to speak in accounts featuring three points, that Hispanic kids tend to structure their accounts by relationship, and that European American kids tend simply to go on. With regard to interdependence, we might especially note the regularity with which Japanese children bring elements Westerners might think extraneous into their accounts: even if expressly directed to focus on one thing—say, how they hurt their foot—they will bring in other times they hurt themselves, or other instances of people being injured. As for interdependence in adult narratives, there are far fewer studies. We do have descriptions such as novelist Leslie Marmon Silko's of Pueblo Indian folktales; these, she writes, are full of repetition, often tied to a certain hill or river, and very definitely nonlinear—"never beginning at the beginning," as she puts it, "and certainly never ending." Still, there is a reason that narrative psychologists typically work with children; after about age nine, narratives tend to become too long and idiosyncratic for definitive analysis.

And so it is that, as we come to the novel and Culture, capital C, I take off my science hat and replace it with another—the hat one wears when one is dealing with the uncertain and the suggestive and all that critic James Wood has called "the bottomless." This is, of course, the novelist's or humanist's hat—wearing which, I find it hard not to wonder about, say, the narrative scaffolding provided by high-elaborative mothers. Does that base structure, timbered by British culture, undergird assertions like Virginia Woolf's in *Moments of Being* that "I find that scene making is my natural way of marking the past"? And—very crucially for those of us engaged in literary pursuits—is this scene-making way of re-membering related to Woolf's transcendent gift for fiction?

We will never, of course, know for sure. But one of Qi Wang's most intriguing findings, that "people who exhibited greater episodic specificity when re-membering the past also exhibited greater episodic specificity when imagining the future" begs the question: do such people exhibit greater episodic specificity when imagining fiction as well? Wang does not address this in her published studies. As I happened to have had a friend in contact with her just as I was mulling this over, though, I was able to send her an email on the subject, to which she most graciously and helpfully replied:

> We have done some work looking at narratives of auto-biographical events and fictional stories and found similar cultural differences: European Americans in-clude more episodic details in both forms of narratives than Asians and Asian Americans. This includes fac-tual as well as subjective details such as thoughts and desires.

And so there it is. The independent self, indepen-dent values, a strong episodic memory, and elabo-rated autobiography are indeed all in line, it seems, with elaborated fiction and—the subject of so much interest among Western critics—the imagining of "subjective details such as thoughts and desires," which is to say, interiority. Does that mean not only that Virginia Woolf really did likely boast a robust episodic memory, but that writers such as Marcel Proust did, too?

With this thought in mind, I looked at the famous opening lines of *In Search of Lost Time*. This is Lydia Davis's new translation:

> For a long time, I went to bed early. Sometimes, my candle scarcely out, my eyes would close so quickly that I did not have time to say to myself: "I'm falling asleep." And, half an hour later, the thought that it was time to try to sleep would wake me; I wanted to put down the book I thought I still had in my hand and blow out the light; I had not ceased while sleeping to form reflections on what I had just read, but these reflections had taken a rather peculiar turn; it seemed to me that I myself was what the book was talking about: a church, a quartet, the rivalry between François I and Charles V.

Again, nothing can be proven. Still, witness the subjective episodic detail everywhere. We get not only the narrator's thoughts, but thoughts he realizes he did not have time to have; and such is the power of thought that it can wake him—even the involuntary thought, ironically, that it is time to sleep. How intriguingly suggestive, too, that, a bit the way a crack Hong Kong chef might serve a bowl of rice gruel as a little nod to his origins, Proust should have opened his opus with a delicious "memory" of remembering that, though fiction, reads like autobiography. He was hardly the first to render his narrative this way, of course; critic Ian Watt notes in *The Rise of the Novel* that it was Daniel Defoe who "initiated an important new tendency in fiction: [the] total subordination of the plot to the pattern of the autobiographical memoir." But never mind—who invented what is not important here. My point is, the whiff of episodic memory suffuses Proust's opus.

That's not to say that there isn't an interestingly interdependent cast to the narrator's sleepy conflation of himself with his reading in this passage, as well as to his absenting himself during long sections of the ensuing work: he disappears into the novel in much the way he describes disappearing into "a church, a quartet, [and] the rivalry between François I and Charles V." All of which could be seen as a sign of an imagination that is part interdependent, part independent, and perhaps is. Most individuals, as we have said, are to be found somewhere along the inter-/independence spectrum, and none is glued to one spot.

Yet should we be tempted to call Proust or his narrator interdependent, we might first ask ourselves how easily *In Search of Lost Time* would translate into, say, classical Chinese? This is a language in which my father would certainly have been able to write his autobiography, particularly well suited as it was to "the recurrent and the typical," as scholar Pei-yi Wu points out in *The Confucian's Progress;* its "terseness, selectivity, and uniformity" were very much in synch with an interdependent self. As for its role in sustaining that self, Wu fascinatingly and suggestively contrasts what early Chinese self-recording we have with the strikingly personal and lively Japanese journals written by women in the Heian period. Barred from the classical Chinese used by educated Japanese men, these eleventh-century writers employed *hiragana,* "a largely phonetic script and a language which, although not completely colloquial, was close to what was spoken in the elegant circles of the capital," with results that may remind us of John Demos's observations about nineteenth-century Americans, and "how much these people, these autobiographers, were writing for their own benefit [and] rather enjoyed the sound of their own voices." As Sei Shonagon avers in *The Pillow Book,* for example, "I merely wrote for my personal amusement things that I myself have thought and felt"—her delightful compendium including innumerable passages such as:

> The day after a typhoon is extremely moving, and full of interest. The lattice and open-weave fences around the garden have been left in a shambles, and the various garden plants are in a miserable state. Great trees have been blown over, and the branches ripped off; it gives you quite a shock to discover them lying there across the bush clover and valerian. Leaves are carefully lodged in all the little spaces of the lattice weave, such a delicate effect that you can't imagine it was the doing of that wild wind.

Never mind that the author of this was unsurprisingly found an irritating "chatterbox" by many in the Heian court (including the presumptive author of the *Tale of Genji,* Murasaki Shikibu, who thought Sei Shonagon "dreadfully conceited"). There is a tremendous unconstrained freshness here, the appeal of which to our contemporary Western taste provides much food for thought.[16] Among the questions raised might be: through what other mechanisms, besides maternal style and schooling and language, does a culture mediate self-making? And might Culture generally serve culture in this way? And has narrative then played a role in sustaining cultural differences for millennia now?

I say "millennia" because of an email I received from scholar David Damrosch, who in response to a question about the Enlightenment and the recognizably modern Western self it fostered, interestingly replied:

> I'd myself say that the differences you identify were already there long before the Enlightenment, certainly for literature, as in the assumption that the Chinese poet is meditating on the natural and social world around him, whereas the Western writer makes things up (the assumption etymologically embedded both in the Latin-based "fiction" and the Greek-based "poetry," both from roots meaning "to make," with connotations in Latin shading over to forgery and deception).

In short: not only is the independent self linked, according to Wang, to making things up, it seems to have been engaged in this, according to Damrosch, even before the words "fiction" and "poetry" were coined. As for the shady connotations of the words that he notes—might writers have been looked on with suspicion not only because they could make the untrue seem true, but because they tended to be highly individualistic, with interests that might or might not be yours?[17] Whatever the case in ancient Greece and Rome, people who made things up were certainly distrusted in the East, as were their products. Scholar Sabina Knight notes that moral objections delayed publication of the first compendium of Chinese fiction for five hundred years—until 1566—speculating that "this delay may testify to fears of fiction's power." And perhaps substantiating those fears, we now have scientific support of a link between individualism and making things up in the work of psychologists Jo Ann M. Farver and Yoolim Lee Shim, who found the play of Korean-American preschoolers to be far more domestic, realistic, and harmonious than the play of their Anglo-American peers, with the latter featuring both more aggression and more fantasy (for example, more dragons and pirates, and so on).

As for the question that some of you are perhaps asking—namely, how do you, Gish Jen, feel about the linking of Asian Americans with low-elaborative mothers and weak episodic memories while European Americans are linked not just with strong episodic memories, but with the episodic specificity of Proust and Woolf? Well, we do have things to talk about in the next lecture. In the meanwhile, though, let me at least point out that not all art proceeds from the independent self.

Witness, for example, Song Dynasty landscapes like Fan Kuan's eleventh-century masterpiece, *Travelers Among Mountains and Streams*. This is a monumental work almost seven feet tall, in which both the looming mountains and endless deep mists dwarf the miniscule mules and their accompanying human figure, said to be a self-portrait. Fan Kuan's signature to the right of the mule train, too, is so hidden by foliage that it was not rediscovered until 1958; and what with these signs of self-diminishment, this scroll, often called the *Mona Lisa* of Chinese art, may not remind us so much of the *Mona Lisa* as of my father's autobiography. Here, though, power—that mountain—is portrayed, not as something from which to retreat, but as something wholly benevolent, and in harmony with nature. Whether this is an idealized portrayal or a reflection of the true state of things—this painting was done during the Northern Song Dynasty, a legendarily harmonious time[18]—the tiny traveler is in any case unperturbed and, we may gather from the mules, well supplied for a long journey. There is no sense that he needs to be larger or to exert more control over his environment, quite the contrary. He ap-

Fan Kuan, *Travelers Among Mountains and Streams.*
Courtesy of the National Palace Museum Collection

Detail, *Travelers Among Mountains and Streams*

pears perfectly content to be a minute, interdependent bit of a magnificent whole.

The interdependent substrate of the painting is clear, too, in a myriad of other ways besides the size of the human figure. The painting uses shifting perspectives rather than a single vanishing point, for example. And in making palpable *qi*—the energy connecting all things—as well as the Daoist ideal of becoming one with nature, this work is hardly about decontextualization. In fact, we could say it is about a radical *con*textualization. Modeling his work after a master named Li Cheng, and employing not only the traditional shifting perspective but traditional forms such as that central massif and an overall tripartite organization, Fan Kuan produced a work that went on, as he likely knew it would, to be much copied and studied in turn. What's more, his dominant achievement was not felt to have been in portraying a singular, transient object, that mountain. Rather it was said to have been in transmitting the spirit of the mountains—in capturing, in other words, an ineffable, eternal essence reminiscent of the sort of scientific phenomena we have associated with interdependence in its Chinese form—field-related phenomena like acoustic resonance and magnetism. This was something he was able to do, people said, by painting like nature itself, purposelessly and without exercise of his will.[19]

All of this makes for quite a contrast with Western art, which, as we've said, seems to have been individualistic from the get go, at least in its literary manifestation, and more often than not remains highly individualistic in its visual form especially. When I went walking with a visual artist friend not long ago, for example, she characterized a concert at the New England Conservatory in which the composer had put bottle caps on the strings of his grand piano as "tame": a visual artist, she said, would have done something much more radical—say, drilled a manhole in the middle of the soundboard, as did an artist at the Museum of Modern Art in New York a few years ago. I don't know how many of you saw this, but the pianist stuck right out through the middle of the strings. She walked around the atrium wearing the piano like a kind of skirt, and playing the keyboard upside down. And this was very much in keeping with the sort of thing one sees in, say, the Venice Biennale—ATMs hooked up to pipe organs, and so on. A visual artist would have done something that made the audience think, my friend said, that would have made the audience question—her clear bias being toward a conception of art that is not so much about simply defamiliarizing the familiar as it is about defamiliarizing the familiar in a liberating way. It is about a thinking outside the box that makes us question, in good individualistic fashion, the box.

This is not unlike conceptions that have reigned for some time now about the novel. I distinctly remember being taught, back when I was a student at Iowa, that all good writing is subversive.[20] And indeed, if society is made of conventions—the many *but, of course*s of life—the novel does tend to put

Performance artist in the atrium of the Museum of Modern Art, New York City. Photograph by Yi-Chun Wu. Copyright © The Museum of Modern Art/Licensed by SCALA/Art Resource, New York.

them in quotes. "But, of course" a single man in possession of a good fortune is in want of a wife. "But, of course" salesmen with trains to make get up and make them and do not turn into beetles. "But, of course" cowboys are not gay. "But, of course" nice Jewish boys do not masturbate with their family's dinner liver. "But, of course" nice Chinese girls do not turn Jewish. These are truths "universally acknowledged." And yet whose truths are they? The novel especially asks, as critic Lionel Trilling has said,

> every question that is forbidden in polite society. It asks us if we are content with our marriages, with our family lives, with our professional lives, with our friends.[21]

That these are not the questions of the stability-seeking interdependent self, but of the troublemaking independent self, I hardly need point out.[22]

And, yes, as with the visual arts, the agenda is liberatory, though it must sadly be said that the idea of artists as liberators is not what it was. For me, the most disconcerting of the Massey Lectures to date may well have been Lawrence Levine's *Highbrow/Lowbrow*, which showed the founding of such cherished institutions as the Metropolitan Museum of

Art in New York and the Museum of Fine Arts in Boston to have been a reaction against the immigrant hordes. So, too, it seems, was the emergence of cultural hierarchy in America—the distinction between highbrow, middlebrow, and lowbrow that, for all its postmodern blurring, continues a cornerstone of art-making today.[23] The late nineteenth-century drive for political order was paralleled, Levine demonstrates, by a drive for cultural order—and this is hardly the only time artistic felicities have turned out complicities. Were we writers to take to heart the reams of theory that have in recent decades shone such a hard light on our best intentions, not to say our best lines, we writers would all have to put our computers up for sale.

That we don't is testimony, I think, to just how powerfully embedded individualism is in our culture, and how much the novel is tied into that, starting with its modus operandi—which, for all its bold confronting of society is, in its own way, determinedly oblique. In keeping with the dominant Western view of "art-art" as proudly, rightly, and essentially useless, that's to say, the novel cleaves to an ideal very similar to that expressed by Archibald MacLeish when he says that "a poem should not mean but be"—a view that could not be more different than that which is traditional and still mostly dominant in China. We might think back to the young Chinese writer who thought of writing as way to make a living from the comfort of her home, for example, or else to figures like the fifteenth-century philosopher Hsueh Ching-chih who, according to legend, once placed a written curse on a tiger terrorizing some villages. As a result, the story goes, the tiger was found dead ten days later—the ostensible moral being that words have power, but that power being, we might note, of a useful nature. That things—even literature—*should* be useful is a given for most Chinese.[24]

In contemporary individualistic America, in contrast, even famously activist writers like the late Grace Paley have maintained that "the writer is nothing but a questioner."[25] That is to say that if novels ultimately help raise awareness of the times and boxes in which we live, it is by a process a bit like the one through which we believe children become effective adults[26]—not by hitching them to one aim or another, but by encouraging the sort of all-absorbing play and "purposeless purpose" with which thinkers like Immanuel Kant and Otto Rank have traditionally associated art. A piece of art, in other words, may be designed. It may evince sophistication and awareness of tradition; it may, like children's play, be positively consumed with society. But in the dominant Western view, it is studiously non-instrumental. Whereas in the East literature with a lesson has traditionally been extolled, in the West the mother of all deadly adjectives is "didactic."[27] Works of art are, rather, like people, autotelic—individuals, in a sense. Like their makers, whom they reflect, they are ends in their very own selves.[28]

And like individuals, they have life. The novel, and especially its characters, are Pinocchio. They are Frankenstein's monster, full of uncanny drive, and, when all is well, they are beyond the writer's control.[29] Every fiction writer worth her salt knows how a character will up and walk off with a piece. You know that to write is as much to give your characters their freedom as it is anything else; and you know that in the end, nothing matters more than that they should breathe and stretch and laugh in your face.

So all right. We read for this, we write for this, we talk endlessly in the contemporary literary world about this. But are our characters and novels truly free, or are they merely one more way in which culture, our supposed enemy, has us in its employ? We have seen that the interdependent self is embedded

in a culture with sources of reinforcement that include maternal style, play style, and schooling style
—eating style, too, by the way. I have not talked
about that, but of course the shared communal
dishes of a Chinese dinner are very much in support
of collectivity, and one more mechanism that helps
check any sliding down the inter-/independent scale
toward independence. So, too, are mass spectacles
such as the opening ceremonies of the Beijing
Olympics in 2008. Not that sliding does not and has
not always occurred: recall Sei Shonagon and her
Pillow Book. But we saw, for example, how classical
Chinese might have served to discourage any stray
Prousts from cropping up; and, though, as open-
minded modern Westerners, we might admire some
examples of interdependent art such as Fan Kuan's
landscape, we in truth mostly shake our heads at all
that reinforcing of a self that in our less guarded
moments we have been known to characterize as ro-
bot- or sheeplike.

Is not the independent self reinforced and policed, too, though? It seems to me that, like signs of
the car culture, reinforcement is everywhere: in the
play of our children, in the number of cereals we can
choose from for breakfast, in the endless promotion
of the single-family house. And think of the hall-

marks of the literary—think of the things we deem sacred: the freedom of our characters, the portrayal of interiority, the focus on the individual. Think of our preference for the elaborated and the fully imagined, and think of our anticipation, if not of the linear, exactly, certainly of the progressive. Think of our extolling of originality and authenticity, with "authenticity" often synonymous with resistance, if not outright hostility, to society; think of our insistence on autotelism. Is it not striking that every single one of these hallmarks is also a hallmark of the independent self? Our idea of the "literary" serves that self as clearly as the Fan Kuan landscape serves the interdependent self, which is to say that the novel seems very much part of a cycle wherein Culture reifies culture.

Of course, that is not all it does; and just as many things bespeak interdependence and yet are not Song Dynasty masterpieces—my father's autobiography, for example—so many things bespeak independence and are not *In Search of Lost Time.* Still I wonder if we "literary" novelists in particular are, like the culture-makers in Levine's *Highbrow/Lowbrow,* only half the liberators we think we are. Perhaps our work slavishly celebrates individualism and the episodic memory far more than we realize, and slavishly contributes, too—by all that we portray in our books and how—to the development of the episodic memory of others. As for whether over-development of that memory correlates with, say, over-tweeting—well, when that study comes out, will we be surprised?

In his essay "Why I Write," George Orwell confidently gave "four great motives for writing" that he feels exist in every writer. The first of these is sheer egotism—to "be talked about, to be remembered after death . . . , etc." The second is aesthetic enthusiasm—an investment "in the impact of one sound on another, in the firmness of good prose or the rhythm of a good story." Then there is historical impulse—the "desire to see things as they are, to find out true facts and store them up for the use of posterity." And, finally, political purpose—a "desire to push the world in a certain direction"—which he finds in every person.

It strikes me today that I must add one more motive to the list, namely fascination with Western narrative. Some of you may know that I participated in an event last year with Joanne Chang, the wizard behind the Flour bakeries in Boston. During this evening she talked about growing up the daughter of Chinese immigrants in Dallas, and how fascinated she was when she went to her friends' houses and discovered that they had this extra course called "dessert." That fascination gave rise to the cookies and pastries we all enjoy today.

Well, Western narrative was for me what dessert was for her. It was America—off limits, alluring, self-indulgent, expansive, brash, antiauthority, obsessed with happiness, and weirdly preoccupied—as Qi Wang might have predicted—with remembering things. And, naturally, it was everywhere—particularly in the predominantly Jewish suburb of Scarsdale, New York, to which my family moved when I was in fifth grade. I'll never forget the playground discourse—so funny, so gory, so exactingly blow-by-blow. And whereas the library at my old school, St. Eugene's in Yonkers, New York, had been a donation library—a windowless one-room affair with dark, sagging shelves and listing, soft-edged discards—the library in Greenacres Elementary School had glass, and air, and lovely, stout shelves packed with new, vertical books, every single one of which I read that first year after our move, including Albert Camus's *The Stranger*—the cover of which I can still recall, with that thick-spoked Algerian sun. (What,

I remember wondering, are "inexecrable cries of hate?") Today, of course, I support efforts to ensure that young readers will see their experiences reflected on the page; but for what it's worth, I myself was not reading back then to "find myself." Rather, I was mostly focused, like an old Singaporean man, on my context. Books were for me an Outsiders' Guide to the Universe, which I read furtively and ecstatically but alphabetically—throwing Camus' Meursault into a kind of mental gumbo with Charles Wallace Murray and Jane Eyre; Miss Havisham was put in to stew with Sherlock Holmes and Lassie. The librarian must have spoken to me many times, but I don't much remember her; I only remember marching out with the books, an armful at time, as if under a spell.

It's an obsession I think about these days, when people talk about Asian and Asian American students and their drive to master the piano, or gymnastics, or math—a phenomenon we touched on in the last lecture. My obsession was different than many, in being wholly my own; and yet, I appear to have adapted for my program an existing cultural template—resulting, eventually, in the writer you see before you. People talk today of being or not being a digital native; I was not a narrative native. The girl who read her school library would never have dreamt of becoming a fiction writer; and it can only be counted ironic that someone focused on her context should ultimately be confronted with that context's focus on the figure—with the independent self enshrined in Western literature.

But there it is. I would not stand here today but for fiction. Change, growth, progression. Scene. Voice. Desire. Individuals who want things, for themselves and for the world—individuals who reach for them. Individuals who cut their hair off, like Jo March; individuals who would "prefer not to," like Bartleby. As a girl, I read and read until I had internalized all that. And then one day I began to write; and . . . well, you know the rest of the story. All of which is to say that the blather one hears about the power of art is apparently true—or some of it anyway. It's complicated. But in at least one instance, a very real bridge between East and West, interdependence and independence, was built of the stuff of fiction.

3

WHAT COMES OF ALL THAT

When we left my father at the end of the first lecture, it was World War II. There he was in college, being bombed by the Japanese in Chongqing; and yet still he and his classmates were studying away just as if "the disturbances were not there." Of course, we have no pictures of this. In envisioning this time in my father's life, though, I have always imagined him and his classmates as a bit like my students when I was teaching English to coal-mining engineers in Shandong province in 1981. They had no library in which to work, so they would simply set their stools out in the basketball court, each facing in a different direction, and sit there for hours. It was truly an honor and a pleasure to teach them.

My students at the Shandong Coal Mining Institute,
studying in the basketball court in 1981

But to return to my father's story—which let me
claim, in interdependent style, to be integral to my
own story, and to the intellectual autobiography I
promised John Stauffer: toward the end of the war
he came to America as part of the war effort, stayed
to do some graduate work, and got caught here by
the Chinese Revolution. The last proved a shock
that took some adjustment. But adjust he did, eventually marrying a woman of some gumption,

namely my mother, who was also here in graduate school. He was pretty lucky to find her. I was in the Museum of Chinese in America in New York not long ago, where I saw the numbers of Chinese immigrating around that time; thanks to anti-Chinese legislation, they were in the low hundreds per year. So if we pause for a moment to envision the two of them at this point, they are happy. She is more literary than he, but he, being an engineer, has not particularly noticed. Never mind that she sat on her father's knee reciting poetry as a girl, my father is busy teaching her things like how to boil water and how to make rice. They go on tours of the grocery store—the white meat is chicken, he explains, the pink meat is pork. And the next thing you know she has sadly left her degree program without writing her dissertation. Instead she has become an elementary school teacher and raised five kids—the second of which is the black sheep, yours truly.

My father, meanwhile, has gotten his doctorate and is now teaching civil engineering at the City College of New York, where he finds that some of the students behave better than others. This is how it is that when, not long ago, I happened to give a reading at CCNY, one of his former students came up to me and told me an amazing story. This

involved a classmate who, having exhibited behavior somewhat divergent from the stool-in-the-
basketball-court model, was asked by my father to
come to the front of the classroom and take out the
garbage. To which the student understandably said,
"What? Take out the garbage?" and so on, until he
finally did it, and returned to the room, only to have
my father say, "Take the garbage back in." To which
the student understandably said, "What?" and so on
again, but finally did it—only to have my father re-
peat, "Take the garbage out"; and when the student
did that, tell him, "Take the garbage back in," until
finally the student was just doing it. He took the
garbage out when my father told him to, and he
took it back in when my father told him to, too. And
then he was allowed to sit down.

It was like a scene out of *The Karate Kid*, if any of
you have seen that movie, and for some of you it
may also recall the tiger mother, Amy Chua, calling
her daughter "garbage." But what is interesting, I
think, is that the student recounting this story,
some decades later, told it with so much affection
and enthusiasm. It was clear, even from this meet-
ing twenty-five or thirty years later, that he wor-
shipped my father—as did, it seems, many other students—and that that story was, in his view, about

life. In fact, according to him, my father's whole course, ostensibly about civil engineering, was about life. But what, we may ask today, was my father teaching them about life? If we try and set aside the self-esteem lens that would simply make this story one about shaming and humiliation, what my father managed to teach them would seem to be something about expectations. Namely, if he could study while being bombed by the Japanese, they could perhaps manage to be a bit more serious.

Also, implicitly, it was about my father's ability—never mind his English—to make his expectations clear. That is to say that by his example, he was giving them the idea that there was agency in what we in the West might think of as self-effacement, but that the Chinese tend to see as self-control. There is a Chinese saying: eat the bitterest of the bitter, become the highest of the high. That is not quite the same thing, but there is a similarity in the thinking—in the interdependent linking of what appear in the West to be polar opposites, and in the idea that one pole engenders the other. This is an idea which animates another moment in my father's autobiography too—one that comes a little later than the section we talked about in the first lecture, and one in which he talks about his decision to stay on past the point where the Chinese government was willing to pay for his ticket back. He wanted to stay because he was just three weeks away from the exams to get his master's degree, he tells us, and figured that if he had to he could "survive by pick up some bread from"—interestingly—"garbage cans."

I will not defend the shaming aspect to his lesson. Whatever the gift to the other students, this experience may or may not have been a gift to the student who was its object; for all we know, he became a criminal. And if we think back a little we may recall that my father himself was raised in a way that brings to mind *The Karate Kid* but also *King Lear.* So let's not take his teaching methods as "the Chinese way" or make it the focus of a pedagogy panel, either.

Still, what we can see is that a lesson in interdependence was being conveyed—that the student singled out was being taught that what he thought about taking the garbage out simply did not matter, or at least not in that context and not at that moment. We might imagine he was being taught blind obedience. We might also imagine, though, that he was being asked to think, like my father in the halls of his house in Yíxīng, Where are we? And, Whose house is this? And, What is the way? rather than

Who am I? And, What do I want? And, Do I feel like doing this? For those of you thinking that there is a Confucian ring to the first set of questions, I would agree. There is an emphasis on the proper order of things that does seem Confucian—proper relationships, too. And for those of you thinking that there is a Confucian but also a Daoist ring to the idea of "a way," I would agree with that, as well. And for those of you thinking that there is an acceptance of naked power here that makes many Westerners uncomfortable, I'd agree yet again. As for those of you thinking that the diminution of the self and the focus on its relationship to its context call to mind the elderly Singaporeans and much more that we talked about in the last lecture: Yes!

Now, this snippet of my father's teaching life reveals something of "what comes of all that"—the subject of today's talk. It reveals something of what can happen when an interdependent culture meets an independent one in an engineering classroom. But our concern, of course, is not engineering classrooms; it is the page. In the first lecture, we saw evidence of the interdependent self everywhere in my father's autobiography. In the second, we saw it in Fan Kuan's monumental *Travelers Among Mountains and Streams* as well, in contrast with which we talked about the independent self, its strong episodic memory, an autotelic view of art, and the elaborated autobiographical and fictional narratives with which they are associated. Does it doom a fiction writer to have grown up, as I did, in an interdependent world, with low-elaborative parenting?

Probably. Still, I have found it heartening to recall Sei Shonagon's *Pillow Book* and the Hokkaido Japanese, and how much the episodic memories of the "little emperors" in China were changed by their environment, even if that last change was in the opposite direction than that desirable for fiction writing. And then there's a book called *Inheriting the City*. I do think I am the only person I know who finds sociology inspirational. However, in it, sociologists Philip Kasinitz, John Mollenkopf, Mary Waters, and Jennifer Holdaway ascribe the strikingly high achievement levels of both Asian and non-Asian second-generation immigrants in New York City to a particular kind of creativity:

> This creativity is evident in the everyday decisions and behaviors of young people who are growing up with a dual frame of reference . . . More than most of us, members of the second generation know that their parents' ways cannot always be their ways. Nor can they un-

reflectively take up . . . American culture . . . Instead, they must choose among the ways of their parents, of broader American society, and of their native minority peers or, perhaps, create something altogether new and different.

The authors go on,

> We often attribute drive and creativity to the self-selection of immigrants or to ethnicity itself, but the real second generation advantage comes from being located between two cultures . . . [in what s]ociologist Ron Burt describes . . . as a "structural hole."

It is clearer from the book than from this quote that life in a structural hole is not an advantage in the way that, say, private school education is an advantage. Still, the larger picture this team describes, including both the "structural hole" in which children of immigrants like myself grow up and the "creative selective assimilation" that results, seems to me on the mark. Are the results of that process as happy for the novel as for, say, cuisine? That remains to be seen.

What it involved in my case, anyway, was incessant reading, as I mentioned in the last lecture—so incessant that I seem to have nudged myself a bit toward the independent end of the inter-/independence continuum, reorganizing my young brain even as I acquired, as readers will, a broadened perspective on the world. My very first and most important teacher at the Iowa Writers' Workshop, James Alan McPherson, has written touchingly about his boyhood experiences in the Colored Branch of the Carnegie Public Library in Georgia, and how "At first the words, without pictures, were a mystery." But then

> They gave up their secret meanings, spoke of other worlds, made me know that pain was a part of other peoples' lives . . . [Until] after a while, I no longer believed in the world in which I lived.

And so it was with me: after a while, I, too, no longer believed in the world in which I lived. I still participated in the spirited and creative maneuvering demanded by life in America for which my father's world of opening and closing doors turned out to be perfect preparation. I shared the family expectation that life was difficult; I shared the expectation that it was full of obstacles. I took out the garbage. But with time I began to realize that while our old world framework had real use, there were possibilities here in America it did not allow us to see.

And so off I ventured into the world of fiction,

sanctuary of the independent self. Multiculturalism was still around the corner by the time I got to graduate school in 1981. Things that undergraduates here and elsewhere had perhaps begun to talk about had not yet reached the culture at large; at Iowa, certainly, no one ever thought to use words like "ethnicity," or "essentialism," or "invention." "Prejudice," though, was very much part of our vocabulary, thanks to the Civil Rights movement, and perhaps that helped me realize that I chafed at some things. This is reflected in, for example, this scene from my second novel, *Mona in the Promised Land:*

> When Mona sits back down, Mrs. Ingle asks, "And where are you from?"
>
> To which Mona answers, surprised, "The same town as you. In fact, Eloise and I are classmates."
>
> Says Mrs. Ingle again, "But where are you from?"
>
> Eloise's brother Andrew glosses this helpfully. "She means where are you from, from."
>
> "Ah," Mona says. And then, with Naomi attending, Mona says, "Deepest, darkest China."
>
> Two of the brothers laugh, but the rest of the family is not sure whether to laugh or not.
>
> "Is that a joke?" asks Eloise.
>
> "Yes," says Mona.

Of course, there were many such moments in my real life as well. I recall the same teacher who told me that all good writing was subversive also telling me, for example, that there was no such thing as a nice writer—and that there was no one so nice as the daughter of an immigrant. To which all I could think was, *Feh. Feh,* too, to the narrative that said Asian Americans were not real Americans—though, well . . . what was a real American anyway? And *Feh* as well to the one that said that Chinese Americans did not write novels, that what we wrote were immigrant autobiographies.[1] As for the idea, once multiculturalism did get underway, that it was now time to embrace my Chineseness, my response was: call me Mona Changowitz.

Through all of this I was aware how much more responsive to my context I tended to be than many of my peers. The Chinese dissident artist Ai Weiwei, in a recent documentary about his life, *Never Sorry,* called himself a kind of chess player, saying that he makes a move, then his opponent makes a move[2]— an assertion that reminded me a little of myself. I once wrote a talk called "Rewriting the Context" describing how, as multiculturalism progressed, books that were impossible one year became possible the next, and how I both seized the new possibilities as they cropped up and sought to speed this process along. My books were in good individualistic fashion driven by internal conflict—"the human heart in conflict with itself," as Faulkner put it—partly because I had learned from my reading that they should be, but partly, too, because I had by this time become well aware of how one might be in conflict with oneself. And if it is not too egregiously self-deluded to say so, it seemed to me that, again as per the artistic agenda of the independent self, my characters were hardly cardboard figures trotted out in service of some didactic purpose. Yet there I was, in interdependent fashion, clearing out a cultural space for myself as well. In this, I was far less accommodating of society than was, say, Shen Fu, if you recall his *Six Records of a Floating Life,* and its description of how rooms could be arranged as were the beds on the stern of a boat, so as not to "have a confined feeling at all." My times were post–Civil Rights, after all. But I did my clearing with a spirit that was, like Shen Fu's, not so much about crusading as negotiating, and driven less by outrage than necessity.

As for that necessity, it is hard today to imagine a time when there was just one Chinese American writer, the great Maxine Hong Kingston, on the scene, and when that seemed altogether natural—when the fact of even a handful of other Chinese American writers having somehow managed to get published was big enough news that we would be featured in *Time* and *People* and more. But such was the case in 1991, when my first novel, *Typical American,* came out. There were many assumptions then, too, about what we were supposed to be writing —a fact that has, of course, not changed entirely. Though the line of scrimmage has moved, the questions Who writes? and About what? are still very much with us.

As for whether I was aware, in any event, that my involvement with my context had Asian roots: I do recall thinking of myself as "borrowing" the landscape the way that Chinese gardens do. (Chinese gardens will, as some of you may know, in holistic fashion incorporate the scenery outside their borders into their design—framing a distant scene, for example, as a way of bringing infinite distance into a limited space, and an element of the real into the garden artifice.) I thought of this use of the context, though, as an aesthetic choice. And perhaps it was indeed an aesthetic choice.

Was it a choice, though, to which I was strongly culturally disposed? I wondered about this when reading a recent online article by writer Luke Robinson about the documentary movie *Meishi Street*, made in 2006 by filmmaker and cultural entrepreneur Ou Ning. Talking about the new digital technology and the group Ou worked with, Robinson says,

> it was the ease with which these cameras could be operated that allowed for the group's particular working practices—a balance between the individual and the collective—to develop. In *Meishi Street*, Ou takes this principle to its logical conclusion. Ten minutes into the film we suddenly discover that the so-called "director" has in fact presented the restaurateur Zhang Jinli with a DV camera: the images, shot in a local park, are clearly taken from his perspective; we can hear his voice off-screen, discussing how to use the equipment, and what to record. As the film continues to unfold in this manner, interweaving Zhang's own footage with that shot by members of Ou's team, it becomes clear that what we are seeing is not simply a collaboration between a group of filmmakers, but a participatory project: a documentary in which the distinction between those in front of and behind the camera has been blurred, the subject of the film actually becoming involved in its production.

"Ou takes this principle to its logical conclusion" . . . Robinson's vocabulary is far more independent than the fascinatingly interdependent devel-

opment he describes. Interesting from an inter-/
independent point of view, too, is the fact that, as
Robinson points out, unlike in Western movies like
director Werner Herzog's *Grizzly Man,* in which the
subject also shoots some footage, who shot what remains unclear in *Meishi Street.* This is an ambiguity
Robinson finds problematic in a way that we might
find itself problematic, what with its underlying assumptions and orientation.

But never mind. Given that in terming some of
my own choices "aesthetic," I have also framed interdependent phenomena in independent terms, I
am hardly in a position to take him to task. Quite
the contrary, what's clear to me today, when I look
at my work, is not only just how much interdependence there was in all this context business, but how
little I myself understood that. Is that really possible?
The lit crits among you are perhaps unsurprised. If
we writers knew everything about our own work,
after all, how would you have stayed in business all
these years? Still, it feels strange to me to think that
until I wrote this lecture I did and didn't know.

In preparing to write this, though, I found myself
looking at the cover of my own first book and being
taken aback: for after all this discussion of, for example, the recurrent and the typical and their association with interdependence, behold, there it was,

the title: *Typical American.* Then I opened my story collection, *Who's Irish?* and was immediately confronted with this passage from a short story called "Just Wait," in which the number two brother in the family, poor Billy, is described as

> Mr. Flea Market in the family as a result of having gone to prep school. No one could explain it, but that's what had happened. He had gone in wearing Nike everything, thanks to money he had made with his paper route, and had come out a 1930s North Woods type who read Herodotus by lantern light. Billy could ice-fish. He talked suddenly slowly. He left off talking after he made his point. That proved the most dramatic change, and the most unnerving, especially as he kept it up all through college and on into what was apparently his adulthood. Now he was forty-two and still doing it . . . Addie's stepbrother, Mark, liked to say that Billy . . . looked as though he had lent L.L. Bean his first tent. And wasn't that some trick for a nice Chinese boy from the wilds of a Boston suburb? In contrast, he, Mark Lee, the youngest of the boys, was Mr. Real World.

Unlike his individualistic brother, that's to say, Mark was not about his inner truth. Rather he

> could predict which streets would get plowed first in a snowstorm, and how long the whole cleanup would

take. He could make sure their street was plowed early—
not so early as to attract attention, but early.

He would have, in short, been perfectly comfortable
navigating the halls and doors of my father's house
in Yíxīng.

As I read on, I saw that there was a flip side to
Mark's comfort in the discomfort felt by others of
my characters when, very much to their chagrin,
they find themselves unable to do their own naviga-
tion. We might imagine the discombobulation of
the old Singaporean men from the last lecture if
the background of a photo were changed, and their
ability to read it, as well—if someone else had to
walk them through it. And so it is, I think, that the
isolation of the independent world is often associated with being shown into that world, as in the
case of the grandmother in the story "Who's Irish?"
who says:

> A daughter I have, a beautiful daughter. I took care of
> her when she could not hold her head up. I took care of
> her before she could argue with me, when she was a lit-
> tle girl with two pigtails, one of them always crooked.
> I took care of her when suddenly we live in a country
> with cars everywhere, if you are not careful your little
> girl will get run over. When my husband die, I promise

him I will keep the family together, even though it was just the two of us, hardly a family at all.

But now my daughter take me around to look at apartments. After all, I can cook, I can clean, there's no reason I cannot live by myself, all I need is a telephone.

This is to say that, contrary to the perception of many in the West, to have an interdependent self is not to have no self. It is to have a different self, the possession of which is a joy; the loss of which is disabling; and the restoration of which can be a joy, too.

I was reminded by this last in rereading a passage about my character Pammie's reaction to life as a single mom in the novella, "House, House, Home." Her new house is tiny and a wreck, but it is legible:

> In it, the family clustered together. The closeness of the arrangement would have driven Sven crazy . . . [but f]or Pammie and the children . . . the house afforded a sense of being almost literally in touch . . . If Pammie closed her eyes during the day, as she often had to . . . she did so with a sense of being able to keep track of what was going on in the house even as she dozed . . .
>
> She missed higher thoughts . . . She remembered conversations she used to have . . . about the figured void, Le Corbusier's Unité d'Habitation, utopianism

. . . [but she loved] the way supper-making filled the consciousness of them all, here—the way they all heard together the *chop-chop* of vegetables being readied for cooking, the metallic *uuhch* of noodles being put in a pot, or the *sweesh* of rice being measured into the rice cooker. Those were sounds that meant steam would be wafting everywhere soon enough, sweet with the smell of meat or sauce. No one needed to be told when supper was ready . . . [W]hen Pammie banged the cooking spoon on the lip of the frying pan that way, a double thump usually, to knock the food off, they knew it had come.

If we think back here to the first lecture, we will not be surprised either by the emphasis on architecture in this novella or by its role in influencing events. The key line in this passage, though, is "No one needed to be told"—so much of the joy of interdependence lying in not having to use words.

Of course, you don't have to have Asian roots to feel dumb joy. One of the passages I remember most fondly from my undergraduate days is the one in Virginia Woolf's *Mrs. Dalloway*, where Clarissa Dalloway describes how the young people at the party

could not talk. And why should they? Shout, embrace, swing, be up at dawn; carry sugar to ponies; kiss and caress the snouts of adorable chows; and then all tingling and streaming, plunge and swim.

It's a wonderful bit of writing. However, I slightly regret having looked it up for this talk as, before I did, I remembered it only for its ecstasy. I forgot that it goes on,

> But the enormous resources of the English language, the power it bestows, after all, of communicating feelings (at their age, she and Peter would have been arguing all the evening), was not for them.

—and that it ends,

> They would solidify young. They would be good beyond measure to the people on the estate, but alone, perhaps, rather dull.

That this is the blithely summarizing sentiment of an independent self, I think you can hear—the sentiment of a self at home with a high-elaborative style and quite sure of the superiority of that. Too sure for my taste today; it's not my favorite Clarissa Dalloway moment. But, well, what a great example this is, at any rate, of how one misreads and misremembers—evidence, perhaps, of my undergraduate self, thrilled to have recognized something in the text but then too dismayed by the disapproval in which it was couched to take that part in. Or did I in fact take it in way back then and only later elide it from my memory—changing it bit by bit over time, the

way Frederic Bartlett's British subjects misremembered the Native American folk tale they were told?
Who knows?

What is clearer is that I am far from the only one
who would reject Clarissa Dalloway's take on the
young lovers. In fact, frequently accompanying the
autobiographical disinterest of interdependent cultures is, at least in Asian cultures, a decided preference for the intuitive and nonverbal, and a strong
association of this with happiness. Cross-cultural
author Christine Gross-Loh and others have suggested that this preference begins in infancy, with
interdependent cultures favoring co-sleeping arrangements and pretend games involving caretak-
ing. Since the advent of the Snugli many have noted,
too, that while more interdependently oriented parents will hold the babies such that they face inward,
toward the parent, more independently oriented
parents will face the children outward, so that they
can see. Independently oriented parents will also
train their children to sleep by themselves, support
the development of abstract reasoning with toys
such as shape-sorters and, above all, promote ver-
balizing as if preparing their children from the start
for participation in a mobile, capitalist, democratic
world.[3] (All of which my husband and I did with our

two kids, by the way, with what appear so far to be happy results.)

In contrast, in my house, growing up, to need to be told something was to have failed, whereas to know something without being told—to understand someone's "heart," especially—was a great thing. Of course, as we may gather from Fan Kuan's *Travelers Among Mountains and Streams* and from the life that Fan Kuan led as a *shānrén*—a mountain hermit—an interdependent person can seek connection with nature. Interdependence does not necessarily mean co-sleeping and reading the minds of others. But still, the horror and *angst* of leaving an interdependent household or group can be considerable. A friend teaching law in Egypt last year reported that people there asked her *sotto voce* if it was true that there are people in America who live alone. And writer Peter Hessler observes in his book, *River Town,* that a

> sense of self [that] seemed largely external [i.e., interdependent] ... was an excellent way to preserve social harmony, but once that harmony was broken the lack of self-identity made it hard to put things back together again. I sensed this whenever I read personal accounts of the victimization during the Cultural Revolution, because these stories were surprisingly full of shame ...

[with] many of these victims . . . racked by shame, clearly believing that they were somehow flawed. It was like a target of McCarthyism immediately breaking down and admitting that he was wrong, or a Holocaust victim hating herself because she was indeed a "dirty Jew."

The reference to shame here brings to mind my father's use of shaming in his classroom and points to a less salutary side of interdependence: group policing can be intense and ruthless. But the joy of a functioning interdependent relationship can be tremendous, too. There are more stories in the newspaper all the time now about immigrants from interdependent cultures who, when given a choice, choose to return, saying that they find America cold and unfeeling; and I'm sure that if he had had a choice, my father, likewise, would have returned to Yíxīng. There's a basic human comfort in interdependence you get a sense of in the painting here by artist Lori Lander, based on a photo of girls in Bali.

To return, ourselves, to the page, though: for all the contentment in my character Pammie's passage, interdependence is often something against which independence vies in my work. Witness, for example, this passage from a new story, called "The Third Dumpster," in which a Chinese American son is try-

Girls, Klungkung, Bali (2010). Painting by Lori Lander, courtesy of the artist.

ing to figure out what to do with his aging parents, who

though they had been Americans for 50 years and could no longer belay themselves hand over hand up their apartment stair rail . . . could not go into assisted living because . . . of the food. Western food every day? *Cannot eat,* they said.

Goodwin had brought them to a top-notch facility anyway, just to visit. He had pointed out the smooth smooth paths, so wonderful for walking. He had pointed out the wide wide doorways, so open and inviting. And the elevators! Didn't they just make you want to go up? He had pointed out the mahjong. The karaoke. The 6-handed Pinochle. The senior tai qi. The lobby was full of plants, fake and alive. Always something in bloom! he said, hopefully.

But distracted as they could be, his parents had frowned undistractedly and replied, Lamb chops! Salad! And that was that.

I should probably point out here that no one ever took my parents to tour an assisted living facility. However, it is true that my mother does not eat lamb chops.

As for what else we might see in this passage—whether we see in its humor a resolution of the tension between independence and interdependence, for example, or just psychic accommodation of the finally irresolvable, I am probably the last person to really be able to say. For what it's worth, though, the humor appears based on a Chinese template. Chinese author Lin Yutang observed in his 1935 classic,

My Country and My People, that the Chinese are given to a farcical view of life, and that

> Chinese humor . . . consist[s] in compliance with outward form . . . and the total disregard of the substance in actuality.

That is to say that what goes with an interdependent disposition, at least in its Chinese manifestation, seems to be a tendency to see regulations, for example, not so much as legitimate constructs with what just might be reasonable, pro-social *raisons d'être,* but rather as so many obstacles in the miniature golf course of life. This attitude will remind us a bit of my father navigating the doors and halls of his house in Yíxīng, and also, perhaps, of the love for cat-and-mouse games of any description we still witness in China today. It is, what's more, related to the cheerful two-facedness of contemporary Chinese manners described in a *New Yorker* article about the Chinese blogger, Han Han, last year. As his publisher patiently explained,

> In China, our culture forces us to say things that we don't really think. If I say, "Please come over to my place for dinner today," the truth is I don't really want you to come. And you'll say, "You're too kind, but I

have other arrangements." This is the way people are used to communicating, whether it's leaders in the newspapers or regular people. All Chinese people understand that what you say and what you think often don't match up.

In short, there is often a reality A and a reality B in China and, unlike in earnest America, an acceptance, even a relishing, of this. The ironies! The gamesmanship! Western observers are often flabbergasted to witness the downright mirthful floating of trial balloons in which people will engage, trying to figure out just what official censors will or will not, at any given moment, tolerate—which is not to say that the limits-testing isn't pained and outraged at heart. It is.

Still, this interdependent navigating can be courageously and brilliantly spirited. Take, for example, artist Ai Weiwei's installation of surveillance cameras in his home last year. He was beaming images of himself onto the internet in protest against government surveillance—a protest that ended, quite deliciously, with the government forcing him to turn the surveillance cameras off. Deliciously, too, he was greeted, at the end of a recent period of probation during which he repeatedly flouted its strictures, with official congratulations: the Chinese government, apparently seeking to avoid publicity, declined to take him to task. Of course, he has yet to win his war. But outcomes like these may remind us of the famous couplet from Chinese novelist Cao Xueqin's classic, *The Story of the Stone:*

> Truth becomes fiction when the fiction's true;
> Real becomes not-real where the unreal's real.

As for whether over-relish of these things can be self-defeating, Lin observed in the 1930s,

> We [Chinese] really look upon life as a stage, and the kind of theatrical show we like best is always high comedy, whether that comedy be a new constitution, or a bill of rights, or an anti-opium bureau . . . We always enjoy it, but I wish our people would sometimes be serious.

And indeed one does wonder whether a culture of gleeful pirating of DVDs and more, such as we see in China today, will ultimately prove self-cannibalizing. Still, it is mostly a relief to "throw off the too heavy burden imposed . . . by life," as Freud puts it, "and win the high yield of pleasure afforded by *humour.*" So it is, certainly, with my character Goodwin, at least, whose transparently cloaked desire for independence—"And the elevators! Didn't they just make you want to go up?"—take a helplessness and frustration that can have no alleviation and turns them into farce.

So much of becoming a writer is called finding one's voice, and it is that; but it seems to me it is also finding something—some tenor, or territory, or mode, or concern—you can never abandon. For some it is a genre like comics. For some, it is a fascination with metaphysics or misfits or marriage. Not that you don't have other interests; but there must be some hat you would not willingly take off. It is the thing that gives a writer, "b.s. artist" that he or she is, at some level, the *chutzpah* to drop the "b.s." It is the source of his or her "authenticity"—this sense that however imaginative a work, the writer has a real stake in it, that he or she is driven by some inner necessity. And if I look back at my own years in graduate school, it seems to me that so much of what my classmates and I were trying to do was to find this thing, trying on and discarding with appalling casualness pronouncements like Lionel Trilling's about how Thomas Mann said that all his work could be understood as an effort to free himself from the middle class, and this, of course, will serve to describe the chief intention of all modern literature.

Feh. Not that I didn't know what Trilling meant about Mann, and not that I didn't admire works like *Buddenbrooks* and, in America, books like novelist Richard Yates's *Revolutionary Road,* with their desire to escape what my architect friend Billie Tsien called "the land of pink and green." I could see, too, that Trilling was right in claiming that there was a more radical agenda—"not merely freedom from the middle class but freedom from society itself"—in much of modern literature.

Having hardly been hemmed in by social mores myself, though—the issues of life in a "structural hole" had more to do with confusion and dissonance—I was far more intrigued by visions like Jim McPherson's of a true, chosen community in which every person's humanity would be perceived. A balance of independence and interdependence, I might say today. But back then I did not have the word "interdependence"; I only knew that I had a reaction to McPherson's vision not unlike the reaction one has when one sees something on Facebook and hits

Like! In related fashion, I warmed, too, to Saul Bellow's diatribe against "artistic" alienation, and what he called the general

> separatism of writers . . . accompanied [as it was] by the more or less conscious acceptance of a theory of modern mass society as . . . a waste land and a horror . . . This [, he went on,] is one of the traditions on which literature has lived uncritically. But it is the task of artists . . . to look with their own eyes . . . They will not, they cannot permit themselves, generation after generation, to hold views they have not examined for themselves.

Like! And then there was John Updike's use of a "fervent relation with the world" as a critical touchstone, when I learned of it—Updike affirming with this a nose-pressed-to-the-glass-ness that seemed to me the opposite of nose-pressed-to-the-mirror-ness. *Like!* As for Susan Sontag's advocacy of an "erotics of art"—a new sensibility, "defiantly pluralistic" and "dedicated both to an excruciating seriousness and to fun and wit and nostalgia"—not sure. Pluralistic was good. Pleasurable was good. "Fun and wit"— very good. "Excruciating seriousness"—well, okay. (I had been raised Catholic, after all, and still liked a good hair shirt.) But was this not a trivializing, consumerist view of art? Growing up as I had, I myself did not need "to see more, to hear more, to feel more"; I was anything but jaded. But perhaps most importantly, her outlook was simply too weighted toward individual experience for me—too much about furnishing the independent self with the goods with which to nurse along its precious uniqueness. *Feh.*

Of course, all of this feeling my way forward led eventually to the novelist I am today—the one I described earlier as concerned with private experience, with questions of love and friendship and family and purpose, but also to a perhaps unusual degree with context-oriented questions like, What doors are open, and what doors closed? And, Whose house is this? And, What is the way? Questions that—because I asked them of the American context—have, despite their Chinese origin, ironically rendered me a distinctly American writer.

As for how a budding writer like me navigated the individualism of so much of Western fiction—I know at least part of the story. To follow which, you need to know that the great god of writing is, of course, Henry James, whose book, *The Art of the*

Novel, was when I was in graduate school, and still is, the Bible. Milan Kundera, meanwhile, the author of another book also provocatively entitled *The Art of the Novel,* is a kind of anti-James. Witness, for example, heretical statements like

> It is a mistake to regard a certain stereotyped structure as the inviolable essence of the novel . . . A novel is a long piece of synthetic prose based on play with invented characters. These are the only limits . . . [T]he novelist's desire [is] to grasp his subject from all sides and in the fullest possible completeness. Ironic essay, novelistic narrative, autobiographical fragment, historic fact, flight of fantasy: The synthetic power of the novel is capable of combining everything into a unified whole like the voices of polyphonic music.

What? I was so shocked the first time I read this passage that I failed to underline the writer's-tip-like statement—"The unity of a book need not stem from the plot, but can be provided by the theme"— that followed. Kundera's novel, after all, was nothing like the realistic artifice focused on the truth of individual experience that arose in eighteenth-century England in the manner described by Ian Watt, but rather some kind of wild throwback, it seemed, to the narratives of Cervantes and Lawrence Sterne. The critical stocks of whom have perhaps risen since the days when they were simple precursors to the real deal—but, well, who cares? The simple fact is that Kundera, back then, made me laugh.

Of course, laughter is a thing I have since learned to take very, very seriously. Even in my callow youth, though, I knew enough to realize that some things let me out of school, and that iconoclastic Kundera was one of them. I will confess here that I don't read him much anymore. Were it not for Kundera, though, would I have laughed out loud as I did, back in graduate school, at H. G. Wells's description of the novels of Henry James? These some of you will recall Wells likened to

> a church lit but without a congregation to distract you, with every light and line focused on the high altar. And there, very reverently placed, intensely there, is a dead kitten, an egg-shell, a bit of string.

This is often quoted to show what a boor H. G. Wells is; even today I feel that I quote it at some risk to my reputation. And do let me point out that James believed himself more catholic than Wells gave him credit for. In a letter to Wells, he in fact protested,

> But I *have* no view of life and literature, I maintain, other than that our form of the latter in especial is admirable exactly by its range and variety, its plasticity and liberality, its fairly living on the sincere and shifting experience of the individual practitioner. [4]

To which Wells interestingly replied on a distinctly interdependent note:

> To you literature like a painting is an end, to me literature like architecture is a means, it has a use.

But be that as it may. All I knew as a graduate student was that I loved and admired works like *The Portrait of a Lady* and *The Wings of the Dove*, but was more at home with what James called "big, baggy monsters"—novels like *Middlemarch* and *Moby Dick* and *War and Peace,* in whose capacious pouches protagonists could be positively misplaced for chapters at a time. I really must say here that I have never read Wells—also that I ended up far closer to James both structurally and on the realism spectrum than I did to Kundera.[5] But I laughed at Wells's description of James, I think, because I felt a dissonance

and because something about Kundera had made
that okay.

I do hate to suggest that any writer can be "explained" by his or her culture; writers cannot be "explained" by anything but a sense of having to answer, somehow, to someone or something no one
else hears. We are simply aurally peculiar. It may en-
rich our experience of Kundera, though, to recall
Richard Nisbett's observation from the last lecture
about how within Europe, individualism intensifies
from East to West, with "the Mediterranean countries plus Belgium and Germany . . . intermediate
between the East Asian countries on the one hand
and the countries most heavily influenced by Protestant, Anglo-Saxon culture on the other." Nisbett
does not talk about Central Europe in particular,
but from Kundera's comments in *The Art of the
Novel,* it seems a fair guess that he stands, if not at
the Far Eastern end of the inter-/independent spectrum, still, somewhere at the interdependent end. I
say this because of remarks he makes, for example,
about how as the novel moves from *Don Quixote* to
Madame Bovary, its focus shifts from the external to
the internal—until "The great illusion of the irre-
placeable uniqueness of the individual—one of Eu-

rope's finest illusions—blossoms forth." The uniqueness of the individual an illusion . . . this is hardly the talk of a diehard individualist.[6]

Moreover, he locates himself and other novelists in a post-Proustian place, saying that

> The time was past when man had only the monster of his own soul to grapple with, the peaceful time of Joyce and Proust. In novels of Kafka, Hašek, Musil, Broch, the monster comes from outside and is called History.

Eschewing interior monologue—insisting that he simply "cannot use" the microphone that, say, James Joyce sets in Leopold Bloom's head in *Ulysses*—Kundera rather investigates, he says, "human life in the trap the world has become." And, of course, the world of the Soviet Bloc was indeed traplike; one can imagine it as having opening and closing doors like my father's house in Yíxīng. Is this why Kundera's characters evince a blinkered focus not unlike Kafka's K., whose thoughts in *The Castle* are, as Kundera points out,

> bent exclusively on the current situation: What should be done then and there, in the immediate circumstances? Go to the interrogation or evade it? Obey the priest's summons or not? All of K's interior life is ab-

sorbed by the situation he finds himself trapped in, and nothing that might refer beyond that situation (K.'s memories, his metaphysical reflections, his notions about other people) is revealed to us. For Proust, a man's interior universe comprises a miracle, an infinity that never ceases to amaze us. But that is not what amazes Kafka.[7]

Of course, Kafka and Kundera are modern writers. But—recalling Shen Fu's *Six Records of a Floating Life* from the first lecture and the "off-center" selves of John Demos's early colonial diaries from the second—I am struck by the similarity of the self Kafka and Kundera portray to selves deemed premodern. It seems to me to point to a self that is finally neither modern nor premodern, exactly, but simply a contingent affair—the modernity of the literature in which it appears lying in the *questioning* of a delimited self, of seeming to be asking, as Kundera puts it,

> What possibilities remain for man in a world where the external determinants have become so overpowering that internal impulses no longer carry weight?

Kundera is clearly conscious that there was a time when internal impulses did carry weight, conscious that they do so "no longer"—conscious, we might say, that an independent self is, ironically, dependent on its context. All of this generated in me, back in graduate school, a very strong *Like!*

I hope it goes without saying that many other writers besides Kundera have mattered to me, too. The focus of these lectures on the inter-/independent self may have a distorting effect a little like the flame George Eliot describes in *Middlemarch* that, held up to a polished surface one knows to be "multitudinously scratched in all directions," cause those scratches to appear to form a "fine series of concentric circles." I have actually loved a huge number of books, starting with *Heidi*, which my godmother sent me one Christmas, followed by *Little Women*— I don't think it a coincidence that when I took a pen name, Gish Jen, it was a spondee, like Jo March. *World and Town* pays deep homage to *Middlemarch*; and I have thought of books from *The House of Mirth* to *Don Quixote* to *The Idiot* to *The Story of the Stone* to *Anna Karenina* far more than I'd ever have expected when I first read them. They have been much more than influences or artistic models; they have been lifelong touchstones. Of course, context-oriented person that I can be, I would hate for the singling out of figures like Elizabeth Bennett and Dorothea

Brooke and Thea Kronberg and Lily Bart to eclipse the enriching and broadening of my world provided by Captain Ahab, and Thomas Sutpen, and Bigger Thomas; but of course, if I had to pick suitemates with whom to enter a housing lottery, they would be from the first list.

To return to my early days as a writer, though: I do think it was crucially heartening for me to intuit via Kundera that the novel could not only accommodate but be enriched by works of a more interdependent orientation. I will say, too, that even as recently as a few years ago, I found myself thrilled when Turkish novelist Orhan Pamuk, in the course of giving the Norton lectures here at Harvard, began complaining about there being too much importance placed on character in Western novels, saying

> People do not actually have as much character as we find portrayed in novels . . . I have never been able to identify in myself the kind of character I encounter in novels—or rather, European novels.

"Furthermore," he went on,

> human character is not nearly as important in the shaping of our lives as it is made out to be in the novels and literary criticism of the West.

And indeed, in thinking about his novel *My Name Is Red*, for example, it is striking how much greater a role the book's puzzlelike architecture plays than the inner depths of its many characters. They seem governed by their context in a way that Pamuk himself notes, insisting that

> More decisive than the character of a novel's protagonists is how they fit into the surrounding landscape, events, and milieu.

More decisive? This is a view that, changeling that I am, I do not share. But never mind. Today, I am happy to report, I do not "need" the fact of Pamuk the way I once needed the fact of Kundera. At the same time, it feels integrating even now to think of ideas of a distinctly interdependent cast aired in Sanders Theatre—something I never would have dreamt of when I was a student.

Meanwhile, if Pamuk and Kundera are proof that you don't have to be Asian to be interdependent, so are various characters in my novels. This is a passage from *World and Town*, for example, involving Carter Hatch, ex-lover of the protagonist, Hattie Kong. At this point, they are still both young neurobiologists; Hattie is working in Carter's lab.

"Don't you see?" Carter would say. "Don't you see?"

There was a Nobel laureate next door to the Hatchery; Hattie was not nice to him because of his prize. Neither was she nice to his minions when they treated others the way they had been treated.

"You forget that you yourself will only be a minion, as you put it, for a while," Carter said. "Do not overinvest in this cause."

And: "Not every grievance is founded, you know. What's your evidence?"

And: "You identify too much with the trod-upon. It's an outsider's outlook."

But she could not help seeing what she saw—people treated as expendable. "They made themselves part of the picture, then get airbrushed out," she said.

Carter shrugged. "This is a lab, not an experiment in living."

"You sound like El Honcho."[8]

"I don't care who I sound like, and may you learn not to care, either."

They had different ideas about integrity. She believed it something in the person; he believed it something in the work. Not that there weren't lines you couldn't cross—there were, absolutely. Still, he thought it important to understand where you had leeway; he thought it better to be effective than noble.

"You're like Meredith," he said once. "More interested in how the world judges you than in what it becomes."

And: "It's a kind of vanity."

And: "You're not on trial."

"Interesting," she said.

"It's important to know your position from yourself," he said.

"Is it."

"Miss Confucius, enough."

She was in training in his lab for now, he would say. When the day came for her to go, she should go. And, they hoped, if they played their cards right, maybe come back as an equal, someday. If not to the university, then at least to the region.

"We must be able to have lunch," he said, several times. "You must agree to be sure of that."

And, of course, she would promise, though she would not have taken either his words or hers too seriously had he not hesitated over his hummus and pita one day and added, thoughtfully and deliberately, "I'll help you."

"If you remember, you mean," she laughed.

But he didn't reach for a carrot stick as she thought that he would. Instead, he looked her square in the eyes and said gently, "I'm going to do everything I can."

And when she laughed again, he said, "Hattie." And, "Don't laugh."

To which she replied, "I'm just trying not to cry, Carter."

And when he put his sandwich down, and wiped his hand, and took her hand for a moment, she accepted it.

And when she got an offer at a far-off lab, she accepted that, too. And when a job opened up in his department, he let her know right away.

"This is just right," he said. "You go away and then you come back. Perfect."

But this is a novel; I don't think I need to tell you it's not perfect. Interestingly, though, it is mostly Carter, not Hattie the outsider, who is defined by his genealogy and by his station. There are moments when things flip, but he is mostly the one intent on reading and negotiating his world, and the one whose journey over the course of the book is toward a more independent self.

This might seem to suggest that the movement from an interdependent to an independent self is always good, or in some way inevitable; and maybe it is, or maybe the narratives we in the West like best simply feature such a movement. In my books, in any case, things are often more mixed. When Mama Wong, in the *The Love Wife,* names her child "Carnegie Wong," for example, she blithely blends independence with interdependence in one fell swoop—pronouncing, in effect, You *will* be a self-made man![9] Is that a progress narrative? And on a macro level, that great staple, American rebirth, has, in *World and Town,* taken on a somewhat complicated aspect, I notice—the typically linear process in which a false self is shed and a true one revealed involving here such a thicket of past, possible, and twinned lives that America comes to seem a bit like a Buddhist temple, only with less incense. It's an America where one can be reborn into the wrong life, for example, and one seems never to have been reborn once and for all; and what does rebirth mean, anyway, for people who've been reborn many times already? As for the American self, it is neither independent, necessarily, nor boundaried, nor stable.

I am often asked to tell my own independence story —the story of how I broke from my family to become a writer, which is to say how, despite having discovered writing right here at Harvard, as an undergraduate in Professor Robert Fitzgerald's prosody class, I nonetheless went through bouts of being prelaw and premed, and was actually attending Stanford Business School when I had my road-to-Damascus moment. This was not as wholly out of the blue as it sounds; I had actually chosen Stanford over Harvard Business School because I knew Stanford had a good writing program. As to whether that showed inner clarity or complete confusion, I will let you be the judge. In any case, I think it fair to say that when I dropped out of Stanford, my parents were not supportive. In this, they were not much different than many Asian or immigrant or working-class parents today—indeed, any parent who perceives the world as dangerous. I might as well have been the errant student at the front of my father's class; in true interdependent style, my parents endeavored in every way possible to get me to take out the garbage.

In response to which, I left their classroom altogether, with predictable results. But one day a Chinese language newspaper, the *World Journal,* ran an article about me on its front page. This identified me as Gish Jen, daughter of Norman and Agnes Jen of Scarsdale, New York—which is to say that, as if following the style sheet from my father's autobiography, they put me, first of all, in generational context. My parents' friends called from all over; and just like that, finally, it was okay. You may imagine how delighted I am that they have been here for all three lectures this week.

And here I am, too, with five books to proclaim my triumphant independence from them—and yet, of course, a debt to them still. I notice, if nothing else, that I can't seem to get away from professors;

teachers and teaching come back again and again in my work. This is a scene, also from *World and Town,* in which Hattie Kong is teaching English to the mother of her new Cambodian neighbors. You need to know that this family, the Chhungs, has moved to northern New England to get away from the problems of the inner city and start over, but that a white van has been coming to town for their son, Sarun. This is unfortunately full of his old gang member friends. What's more, a blue car has been coming around for the Chhungs's daughter, Sophy. That is being sent by some Christian fundamentalists.

"Tie?" asks Mum.

"*Tea,*" says Hattie. "Yes, I would love some *tea.*"

Mum fills a white enamel saucepan with water and offers Hattie some dried anchovies.

"Thank you. Delicious." Hattie has always loved little fish—salty sweet things, too. "Thank you," she says again.

Mum's head bobs.

"You should say, You're welcome."

Mum tries.

"You're welcome," Hattie says again.

"Y-oh wer-cum."

Hattie's mother may have been a heretic, but still,

when Hattie was a girl, her English lessons were based on the Bible. She can still see her old green primer with the cross on its cover. And inside—all those bearded foreign devils with helmets on their heads—she can see them, too. Still, it was a textbook; Mum should probably have a textbook. For now Hattie simply runs through the vowels, noting problems.

"Can you say bait?"

"Bay," says Mum.

A bit of twang there; trouble with the ending consonant.

"Can you say 'bat'?"

"Bat."

Hattie makes a note. "Beet?"

The next lesson, Hattie works on pronunciation again, but adds some phrases: Thank you, Thanks, You're welcome, How are you. The sounds are hard for Mum, but she smiles the whole time, tentative but eager. Learning English at her age is not easy; she might as well try to *tuck Mt. Tai under her arm and jump over the North Sea,* as Hattie's father used to say. Still, she reminds Hattie of how the students make the teacher. Mum is such a different student than Sophy, but then her students were all different, she remembers. And how each one gave her a bit of herself; she remembers that, too. She looks forward to coming again.

The third lesson, Gift is awake and hurling things. Having just discovered that he can walk and throw

things at the same time, he picks up the remote control
and throws it. Next, a bottle opener. Next, a bunch of
keys. A-meh! he shouts, A-meh-a-meh-a-meh. His chest
is streaked with drool, his face bright with naughty de-
light. Still, Mum calmly sets out a dish of dried mango,
leaving it to Chhung to make loud scary noises—*hecq!*
hecq! He leans forward, raising a threatening hand. Gift
just laughs.

Mum frowns.

"Do you want to meet another time?" Hattie asks.

Chhung shouts. Gift goes running out of the room,
his diaper hanging half off. Meh-meh-meh! Chhung
glowers; Mum leans forward—to comment on all this,
Hattie thinks. But, no.

"Why," she says. "Caa."

Hattie thinks. "The white car? Is it back?"

"Flen," Mum says. She closes her eyes, shaking her
head.

"You are worried about Sarun. His friends."

"Wor-ry," she says clearly. A word she knows.

"He's upsetting your husband."

Mum nods, pensive. She presses hard between her
eyes with her thumbs, her other fingers spread-eagled,
then lets her hands fall to the table. "Ch-eye?"

"Child? Me? Yes. I have a son."

"He-ah?"

"Here? No," says Hattie. "He lives far away. Far far
away."

"Gone?"

"Gone? Yes. He's gone."

Mum takes this in. Her face is smooth as a girl's, but her glance is a mother's glance, appraising and thoughtful.

"Chiddt gone," she says. "No . . ." she hesitates.

"Stay?"

"Sday," says Mum. "No sday."

"Do children stay in Cambodia?"

Mum nods.

"It's hard here, you're right. The children don't stay."

"Mod-aa, fad-aa . . ." Mum stops.

"Yes. Mother, father are alone here. The children don't stay. The children go." Hattie speaks clearly and slowly. "The children go."

"You, sef?"

"Do I live by myself? Yes."

Mum shakes her head. "Ha."

"Yes, it's hard. Quiet." Hattie continues to speak clearly. Slowly. "You do everything yourself. Decide everything yourself." She smiles a little though she can see it would be all right if she didn't—that it would be all right with Mum. "Some people like it but I find it hard."

"Ha," Mum says sympathetically. "Sarun."

"Sarun."

"Why. Caa."

"Sarun is getting in the white car."

"Sophy."

"Sophy, yes."

"Brew. Caa."

"Sophy is getting in the blue car."

Mum shakes her head.

"It's hard." Hattie doesn't know what else to say. "I'm sorry." They should really work some more before Gift comes back. And Hattie has a lesson book for Mum in her bag; she should get it out. But instead they just sit a moment—two women at the same table.

You can hear in this passage, I think, how hard the individualism of American life is for Hattie and Mum—though, harkening back once more to some of what we talked about on the first day, we all, I suspect, have some of their conflict in us.

We talked in the last lecture about Western art, and Kant's purposeless purpose, and about art's ability, despite its insistent uselessness, to think outside the box in a way that helps us see the box. So is there a box in your work, Gish Jen, you might reasonably ask, and if so, what is it? To which I would answer that a number of social constructions have come in for scrutiny in my books—among them, Americanness, ethnicity, the family, the nation, the natural, and the idea of rebirth. And, of course, what Thomas Hardy called a "revolt against accepted things" is to be found in this.

But I have also been looking at the boxes within—at the worlds we make of the world and why, and at the cultural constructions that are the independent and interdependent self. This has only been half-conscious, but if you were to ask me, Am I ambivalent about individualism? The answer is clearly, yes. You can see this even in the way the intellectual autobiography in these lectures has resisted a "natural" focus on the self. While less context-focused than, say, my father's autobiography, mine is nonetheless perhaps more context-focused than John Stauffer might have expected.

As for whether we will be seeing more work like this, my guess is that we will. The underlying ambivalence is, after all, as I said in the first lecture, shared by more all the time, both abroad and at home. Whether our domestic ambivalence is a product of globalization or native communitarianism or both is hard to say for sure. But in any event, the frequency with which one hears the word "community" these days is astounding; the word "alienation" seems to have lost the association with authenticity it had in, say, Holden Caulfield's time; and I could not help but notice that, at my daughter's graduation from middle school, the principal quoted from a song by Fleet Foxes called "Helplessness Blues." The lyrics to this went:

> I was raised up believing I was somehow unique
> Like a snowflake distinct among snowflakes
> Unique in each way you can see
> And now after some thinking I'd say rather be
> A functioning cog in some great machinery
> Serving something beyond me.

The Forty Part Motet by Janet Cardiff, installation view at MoMA PS1, 2011. Reprinted with the permission of the artist, MoMA PS1, Luhring Augustine, New York, and Galerie Barbara Weiss, Berlin.

What's more, not too long ago at the hip MOMA extension, PS1, in New York, artist Janet Cardiff mounted an exhibit that consisted of forty speakers set in a circle in a large room. From each speaker projected an individual voice, whose words you could clearly hear if you stood close to it; yet from the middle of the room you could not make these out at all, only the great glorious wash of sound that was *Spem in alium,* an overwhelmingly beautiful, forty-part motet written in the sixteenth century by composer Thomas Tallis.

All of this is to say that when, in a recent article in *Daedalus,* critic Michael Wood wrestled with the possibility that narrative self-articulation is not for everyone, and with philosopher Galen Strawson's claim that "the business of living well, for many, is a completely non-Narrative project," he was hardly alone. There's been a welcome expansion of our cultural menu.

However, as a person who, as I said in the beginning of these talks, embodies a dialectic, I sometimes find that I am not altogether delighted by this expansion. I was perfectly happy at the PS1 exhibit, and I was perfectly happy reading the Wood and Strawson pieces on this subject. Yet I find that I cannot read articles unqualifiedly extolling interdepen-

dent values without wanting to ask where we would
be as a society if we did not value voice and democracy
and event and the extraordinary. To this you will say,
*How perverse! Individualism has produced some serious
perceptual distortions. It has promoted de-contextualization
and isolation; it has promoted narcissism. It has promoted
arrogance. It has promoted a disembodied reason. It has
promoted a culture that so celebrates uniqueness that people are driven mad trying to prove themselves unique.*

True. However, individualism has also contributed critically to the security and leisure that enable
people to imagine lives where they can elect to focus on the relational and contextual and unextra-
ordinary. In beholding, sometimes, the New Age
embrace of Buddhism, for example—that ultimate
interdependent religion—I find it hard not to think
of Cambodia, and how Buddhism opened the door
there to disaster. As a Cambodian friend once told
me, a country needs two wheels. One is the wheel of
dharma, and the other is the wheel of law. This is a
version of what John Demos said, too, at the end of
Circles and Lines—that we need both the circle *and* the
line. And indeed that, now, seems to me exactly
right. We need both the interdependent and the independent self. But how interdependent of me to

see them as two poles of human experience that cannot be disengaged!

As for the perennial question of whether the literary novel is dead—related as that is to the question of whether there really is a special value in play and purposeless purpose, and all we talked about vis-à-vis Western art in the last lecture, I think you can see from much of what I've said today how much more the novel knows than the writer who wrote it. In an email, Qi Wang with extreme graciousness said that my novel, *Typical American,* foreshadowed much of the next twenty years of psychological research into the inter- and independent self; and of course, I wish I could take credit for that. Ironically, though, I must mostly credit that great individualistic invention, the novel. Has creative selective assimilation played a role here, too? Have I not, in classic second-generation fashion, taken the novel culture from my American context and crossed it with elements from my parental culture? Yes.

Still, let me say that I recognize something in these lines from poet Czeslaw Milosz. He didn't write them about the novel, but he could have, because true as they are about poetry, they're true of the novel, too. The lines are from "Ars Poetica?":

In the very essence of poetry there is something
    indecent;
A thing brought forth that we didn't know we
    had in us,
So we blink our eyes, as if a tiger had sprung out
And stood in the light, lashing his tail

And that's exactly right—for the novel, too, they're right. It brings things forth that we didn't know we had in us. We blink and see a tiger; and then there it is, sprung clean out and standing in the light.

If I may tell one more story about my father, it is about his last days before his retirement at CCNY, and how he was enjoying a huge surge in popularity on campus, which the other professors could not help but notice. "So, Norman," said one, "I notice all the students are waving at you so happily. Why is that? What is going on?" To which my father replied, "You know why they are happy? Because I gave them all A's"—an answer that surprised the professor making the inquiry, since my father was, as you might imagine, a famously tough grader. But when he looked at the class list, there it was: my father really did give every last student an A.

It was for him a way of "making some joke," as he liked to say—his way of saying, I'm taking my hat off now, and you know, it was just a hat. A very interdependent view, related to all we've been saying about humor, and gamesmanship, and role-playing: it's as if he were saying, it's important to know your role, but it's important to know, too, that it's only a role. And there lies wisdom, we might say . . . though what about the thing I searched so hard to find as a young writer at Iowa? The thing I could never abandon—the hat I could never take off?

Well, never mind. Let me just say in closing that it has been a pleasure and a privilege to stand here as I have these three days, wearing the Massey hat. I take it off now, though, with pleasure, too.

Thank you all so much for listening; you have been a dream audience I will always remember. If I could, I would give every one of you an A.

Notes

1. This was the "New Century, New Literature" conference at the Fairbank Center at Harvard in 2010.

2. To quote that old windbag, Polonius.

3. I will also use the word *episodic* as psychologists do, as a way of designating a kind of memory. *Episodic* as used by English majors, in contrast, refers to the kind of loose-knit narrative that characterized, for example, picaresque novels—narratives with an un-Aristotelian, "and then, and then" feeling.

1. MY FATHER WRITES HIS STORY

1. Please note that while my father's text is clearly Chinese, I make no claims that this sort of Chineseness is more Chinese than any other kind.

2. Some months after I wrote these lectures, I discovered that this date is actually wrong. My father, unbeknownst to himself, was born, not on the 26th day of the sixth lunar month, but on the 23rd day of the sixth.

3. *Rén* is the pinyin Romanization for our last name; the same character is romanized in the Wade-Giles system, "Jen." Also, reinforcing the idea of a self as a relational rather than an independent entity, my father had at least two other Chinese names—a "milk" name used by his parents and an everyday name used by friends and schoolmates. He acquired an English name, Norman, as well, when he came to the United States, along with several nicknames, and never much cared what anyone called him in any case.

4. My three brothers are named Rén Qīng Dà, Rén Qīng Huái, and Rén Qīng Yuán.

5. There was an effort to coordinate the names of the girls, with my second uncle's oldest daughter, my fifth uncle's two daughters, and me all given names that begin with *bì*. The intention behind this is unclear, and there seems to have been some confusion about which character for *bì* to use: my fifth uncle's two daughters were given names with characters that had the same sound but a different meaning than the character used for my name and that of my oldest cousin. This may be a reflection of the chaos of the time.

6. These shops appear to have been the main source of food for these towns.

7. "Which we never was there" is a common expression of my father's. He means that he never even saw the second floor of his grandfather's enormous suite.

8. These small worlds are reminiscent of the many retreats one sees portrayed in Chinese paintings. An association of space with a modicum of personal freedom is also an unsurprising theme in contemporary Chinese interviews such as those collected in a book called *The Chinese Dream*.

9. My father's desire to become a monk in the mountains was the subject of one of my earliest literary efforts, a poem I wrote while an undergraduate.

10. Though her father was named Hsu, her mother was apparently a Jen; this kind of intermarriage was not uncommon at the time. Her name in Pinyin is Xú Bǎochū.

11. By "real event" I mean an event that precipitates other events.

12. His mother and other family members were not in Shanghai.

13. Just as interdependent views of art stress practice and mastery over the heeding of a divine spark within, interdependent views of academic achievement stress discipline and effort over innate talent.

14. My father's emphasis here on an ability to read the context recalls his earlier praise for his mother.

2. ART, CULTURE, AND SELF

1. Self-sacrificing as this self can be with regard to its own group, it can be brutally hostile to outsiders.

2. The study involved ninety-five subjects from a variety of Asian countries, including China, Korea, Pakistan, India, and Vietnam. Their average age at immigration was around four; they were around twenty years old at the time of the study.

3. The focus of the study was episodic memory—a term we will explore in a bit. The subjects were therefore instructed to focus on and record particular events rather than routine activities.

4. We should note, however, that nonintrospective Chinese writings, from *The Water Margin* to the work of contemporary novelists such as Yu Hua and Mo Yan can be outrageously uninhibited—the literary output, perhaps, of the interdependent self in its navigatory mode.

5. In this as in most of the East–West studies cited, American-born Asian Americans tend to test somewhere between the two extremes.

6. The authors of the study were Joshua Goh, Michael W. Chee, Jiat Chow Tan, Vinod Venkatraman, Andrew Hebrank, Eric D. Leshikar, Lucas Jenkins, Bradley P. Sutton, Angela H. Gutchess, and Denise C. Park.

7. The more holistic Asian orientation seems to me related not only to a general orientation toward groups and grouping, but to a tendency to see context as greatly in-

fluential. This is in turn partly due to the Asian conception of the self as permeable. As an old Chinese adage
goes, if you are near red, you will turn red; if you are near
black, you will turn black; and every Chinese grows
up hearing how the exemplary mother of the Chinese
philosopher, Mencius, moved three times to find the
right environment for her son. Environment is believed
critical.

The interdependent self, what's more, tends to be
a bit like a farmer endlessly scanning the sky. Writer
Evan Osnos observes in a recent *New Yorker* blog post, for
example, how "In the domain of business and government relations, a company, regardless of how private it
is, can be called to provide sensitive proprietary information [including encryption codes] . . . at any time . . . As
. . . the China technology and security expert at the
Council on Foreign Relations put it . . . 'Private compa-
nies in China are always wondering what the government is going to want next.'" And this is, of course, just
one of innumerable examples of the way the context
makes itself felt, and why a certain outwardness of focus
might be warranted.

8. The abstract from Shinobu Kitayama, Keiko Ishii, Toshie
   Imada, Kosuke Takemura, and Jenny Ramaswamy's
   study reads:

   Hokkaido was extensively settled by ethnic Japanese
   beginning in the 1870s and for several decades there-
   after. Many of the current residents of Hokkaido are
   the descendants of the original settlers from this period. As predicted, Japanese socialized and/or im-

mersed in Hokkaido were nearly as likely as European Americans in North America to associate happiness with personal achievement . . . , to show a personal dissonance effect wherein self-justification is motivated by a threat to personal self-images . . . , and to commit a dispositional bias in causal attribution [the fundamental attribution error].

9. For those of you wondering how psychologists can measure something like individualism, the answer is via a number of indices, the best known of which is probably the fundamental attribution error mentioned above. This is a measurable tendency to ascribe more credit to an individual for a given outcome, and less to situational factors, than is objectively appropriate. For example, in a classic experiment, a group of essayists were randomly assigned pro- and anti-Castro positions. The results were then given to a group of readers, some of whom, when they were later told of the experiment and the assignment, readily accepted the truth. Readers from individualistic cultures like the United States, however, tended to erroneously insist that the essays "had" to reflect the writer's true feelings. This result has been duplicated using less politically charged content as well, and is reflective of the undue stock the highly independent self places in individual agency.

10. Nisbett particularly notes the "weakened commitment to the family and other in-groups coupled with a greater willingness to trust out-groups and have dealings with their members" brought about by the Protestant Reformation. Protestant values were, what's more, "intensified

in the Calvinist subcultures of Britain, including the Puritans and Presbyterians."

11. From Ralph Rusk's footnote to a letter from Emerson to Margaret Fuller, February 1847. Thanks to biographer Megan Marshall for this tidbit.

12. Paternal style probably matters as well, but in the populations under study, mothers did the bulk of the parenting.

13. In the words of one young Asian American quoted in a study of second-generation immigrants called *Inheriting the City:* "Chinese parents don't really talk to their kids . . . They're very strict and they hit you if you're bad and I'm watching television and I'm seeing the white parents talk to their kids and I'm like why don't I get that? Why don't I get encouragement and like, why don't they tell me stuff?"

14. That Asian mothers do not have a corner on low-elaborative conversation is suggested by the fact that here in Cambridge, Massachusetts, Cambridge Hospital distributes free baby bibs that say, "Talk to Me!" to all mothers. The population they serve is not particularly Asian.

15. As Jerome Bruner notes, "much of self-making is based . . . on the apparent esteem of others, and on the myriad expectations that we early, even mindlessly, pick up from the culture in which we are immersed."

16. Also suggestive of an association of classical Chinese with the suppression of autobiography is the fact that

although the preface to Chinese writer Lu Xun's famous "Diary of a Madman" uses classical Chinese, the diary excerpts employ the vernacular, *bái huà*. A fascinating blend of independent and interdependent elements, this story ends on an interdependent note, with a call to "Save the children . . ."

17. This is still a concern today. As any relative of a novelist can tell you, there is always a worry that said novelist will someday turn family matters into an advance.

18. That all may not be total harmony, and that there is an inherent rebuke of Confucianism in things Daoist is suggested by the lines in the Daoist classic, the *Dao De Jing:*

> The highest virtue is to act without a sense of self
> The highest kindness is to give without a condition
> The highest justice is to see without a preference
> When Dao is lost one must learn the rules of virtue
> When virtue is lost, the rules of kindness
> When kindness is lost, the rules of justice
> When justice is lost, the rules of conduct

However, a portrayal of an ideal such as Fan Kuan's may or may not have been a critique of society per se, and in the peaceful, prosperous Northern Song dynasty syncretism was the order of the day.

19. This purposelessness is exactly the opposite of Kant's purposelessness, which we will discuss shortly. Though artists like Fan Kuan endeavored to cultivate a state of mind such that the work emerged without exercise of will, the resulting work typically conveyed moral lessons

or other didactic content. Kant's ideal artist, meanwhile, was imagined to design his or her work quite deliberately. Ultimately, though, the result presented neither ideal nor lesson; it was simply art for art's sake.

I might point out, too, that Fan Kuan's painting without will or effort is as interdependent a phenomenon as the fiercely navigatory self we discussed earlier in these lectures. The difference is that Fan Kuan, who lived as a hermit in the mountains, stresses a certain Daoist receptivity and other-worldliness.

20. I was taught this by novelist Lynne Sharon Schwartz, who had a quote from Thomas Hardy up in her office. This read, "Literature is the written expression of revolt against accepted things"—a notion shared by many, including critics Matthew Arnold and Lionel Trilling.

21. In addition, the novel encourages us to feel empathy for many exemplary and eventually-to-be-exemplary types, such as Emma in *Emma,* but also many unsavory and disreputable types—antiheroes like the bum in Knut Hamsun's *Hunger,* for example, who you just know did not bring his number 2 pencil to his SATs given that in the novel he almost eats his pencil.

22. Far from emphasizing the inextricability of the self from its context, fiction has actually aimed at times to liberate the self once and for all. As Trilling put it in *Beyond Culture,* Thomas Mann

> once said that all his work could be understood as an effort to free himself from the middle class, and this, of course, will serve to describe the chief intention

of all modern literature. And the means of freedom which Mann prescribes . . . is the means of freedom which in effect all modern literature prescribes. It is, in the words of Claudia Chauchat, *"se perdre et meme . . . se laisser deperir,"* and thus to make plain that the end is not merely freedom from the middle class but freedom from society itself.

We will come back to this quote in the third lecture. In the meanwhile, I should point out that this is an idea about which even Trilling finally proved ambivalent; and today alienated authenticity is far less fashionable than interconnectedness. At the same time we might note that in popular movies such as *Avatar,* opting for inter-connectedness still entails a violent confrontation between individual authenticity and evil society—and ultimately, yes, an escape from societal bonds. It remains, in short, an independent narrative.

23. Should you imagine that these categories have been done away with, you have only to think *women's writing* to realize they have not. I might add here that there are links between gender, interdependence, and literary achievement that seem to me worth exploring.

24. I should really say, not "even," but "especially" literature, as the inherent moral modeling that stories can provide speaks to two deep Chinese beliefs. The first is that imitation is innate; and the second, that bad outcomes are best headed off by zealous tending of people to make sure that, like trees, they grow up to be healthy, straight,

and, like the stories, useful. Stories have thus been seen as a civilizing force for millennia. Of course, in contemporary fiction, the portrayal of the exemplary, identified as it came to be with socialist propaganda, has waned. However, Chinese novels are still typically more pointed and less exalted in purpose than in the West.

25. It's true that the novel can offer important insights into the *zeitgeist*. Works like, say, Nadine Gordimer's *July's People* or Robert Musil's *Confusions of Young Törless* are esteemed, though, not only for those insights but for how they are rendered: namely, through what Henry James called the "present palpable intimate"—i.e., individual experience.

26. At least in middle- and upper-class America.

27. Overtly pointed books are scathingly dismissed even by those at some level indebted to them. The upshot of *Uncle Tom's Cabin,* for example, was put by James Baldwin as, "This is perfectly horrible! You ought to be ashamed of yourselves."

28. The disinterestedness of art has been attacked by Nietzsche, Freud, Marx, and a myriad of others, and yet still informs contemporary mainstream ideas about fiction.

29. As for the source of this energy, no one knows. But supporting the idea that it may be fundamentally linked to the independent self, psychoanalyst D. W. Winnicott suggests it to lie in "the potential space" formed by the separation of a child from its mother. This, he said, is

at first filled with a transition object—a teddy bear or a blankie—a thing "presented from without," as he put it, yet infused with feeling from within. I know teddy bears are not the first thing we think of when we think of art. But this is his oddly persuasive claim, as is the notion that later in life, this space becomes the charged zone of culture, including theater, music, and writing. It is the zone of reading, too, which everyone knows to be one part text and one part what the reader brings to it, often to the horror of the author.

3. WHAT COMES OF ALL THAT

1. I began *Typical American* while on a fellowship at what is now the Radcliffe Institute but was then the Bunting Institute, where I was constantly asked if I wasn't writing an immigrant autobiography. This was something Maxine Hong Kingston had, some years earlier, been assumed to be writing, too (with the result that *Woman Warrior,* originally intended as fiction, was published as nonfiction). Today we may realize this assumption to be an interestingly complicated one.

2. His opponent being the Chinese government. Many contemporary Chinese writers would probably say something similar.

3. In China, some version of the latter model may come to dominate in the future. An intriguing study in Shanghai and Beijing by X. Chen and colleagues showed that whereas shy, "good citizen" children were popular and

viewed as competent and likely to become leaders in 1991, by 2002, when the market economy had taken hold and individual initiative had become critical, shy children were unpopular, and viewed as incompetent and unlikely to become leaders. This study does not prove that maternal and schooling practices, etcetera, will change whole hog; Chinese society remains an authoritarian and overcrowded one, in which context-sensitivity will remain adaptive. Still, some change is possible.

4. This letter is dated 10 July 1915.

5. I seem to have, though, like Kundera, a liking for multipart structures (such as these lectures).

6. Kundera also embraces many aesthetic preferences typically felt to be Eastern—witness his interest in ellipsis, economy, and the ying-yang like beauty of weighty themes conveyed with lightness, for example. His strong aversion to autobiography also brings to mind the autobiographical disinterest associated with the interdependent self.

7. Interestingly, Ai Weiwei also cites *The Castle* in a 2011 *Newsweek* article called "The City: Beijing."

8. "El Honcho" is Carter's father.

WORKS CITED

Ai Weiwei. "The City: Beijing." *Newsweek*, August 28, 2011.

An Dun. *The Chinese Dream: Real-Life Stories of the Common People in Contemporary China*. Beijing: New World Press, 2009.

Austen, Jane. *Emma*. Boston: Little, Brown, 1901.

Baldwin, James. *Notes of a Native Son*. Boston: Beacon Press, 1984.

Bartlett, Frederic C. *Remembering: A Study in Experimental and Social Psychology*. Cambridge, England: The University Press, 1932.

Bruner, Jerome. "Self-Making Narratives." In *Autobiographical Memory and the Construction of a Narrative Self*, edited by Robyn Fivush and Catherine A. Haden. Mahwah, N.J.: L. Erlbaum, 2003.

Cao Xueqin. *The Story of the Stone*, vol. 1: *The Golden Days*. Translated by David Hawkes. New York: Penguin, 1973–1986.

Chen, X., G. Cen, D. Li, and Y. He. "Social Functioning and Adjustment in Chinese Children: The Imprint of Historical Time." *Child Development* 76 (2005): 182–195.

Chua, Amy. *Battle Hymn of the Tiger Mother.* New York: Penguin Press, 2011.

———. *World on Fire: How Exporting Free Market Economy Breeds Ethnic Hatred and Global Instability.* New York: Doubleday, 2003.

Demos, John. *Circles and Lines: The Shape of Life in Early America.* Cambridge, Mass.: Harvard University Press, 2004.

Domino, George, and Mo Therese Hannah. "A Comparative Analysis of Social Values of Chinese and American Children." *Journal of Cross-Cultural Psychology* 18, no. 1 (1987): 58–77.

Douglass, Frederick. *Narrative of the Life of Frederick Douglass.* New York: Chelsea House, 1988.

Emerson, Ralph Waldo. *The Letters of Ralph Waldo Emerson,* vol. 3. Edited by Ralph Rusk. New York: Columbia University Press, 1966.

Farver, Jo Ann, and Yoolim Lee Shin. "Social Pretend Play in Korean- and Anglo-American Preschoolers." *Child Development* 68, no. 3 (1997): 544–556.

Gladwell, Malcolm. *Outliers.* New York: Little, Brown, 2008.

Goh, Joshua, Michael W. Chee, Jiat Chow Tan, Vinod Venkatraman, Andrew Hebrank, Eric D. Leshikar, Lucas Jenkins, Bradley P. Sutton, Angela H. Gutchess, and Denise C. Park. "Age and Culture Modulate Object Processing and Object-

Scene Binding in the Ventral Visual Area." *Cognitive, Affective, & Behavioral Neuroscience* 7, no. 1 (2007): 44–52.

Gordimer, Nadine. *July's People.* New York: Viking Press, 1981.

Hamsun, Knut. *Hunger.* Translated by Robert Bly. New York: Farrar, Straus and Giroux, 1967.

Hessler, Peter. *River Town.* New York: HarperCollins, 2001.

James, Henry. *The Art of the Novel: Critical Prefaces.* New York: Scribner's, 1937.

——. *The Letters of Henry James,* vol. 2. Edited by Percy Lubbock. New York: Charles Scribner's Sons, 1920.

Jen, Gish. *The Love Wife.* New York: Knopf, 2004.

——. *Mona in the Promised Land.* New York: Knopf, 1996.

——. *Typical American.* Boston: Houghton Mifflin, 1991.

——. *Who's Irish?* New York: Knopf, 1999.

——. *World and Town.* New York: Knopf, 2010.

Kant, Immanuel. *Critique of Judgment.* New York: Hafner, 1951.

Kasinitz, Philip, John H. Mollenkopf, Mary C. Waters, and Jennifer Holdaway. *Inheriting the City: The Children of Immigrants Come of Age.* Cambridge, Mass.: Harvard University Press, 2008.

Kim, Heejung, and Hazel Markus. "Deviance or Uniqueness, Harmony or Conformity? A Cultural Analysis." *Journal of Personality and Social Psychology* 77 (1999): 785–800.

Kitayama, Shinobu, and Dov Cohen, eds. *Handbook of Cultural Psychology*. New York: Guilford Press, 2007.

Kitayama, Shinobu, Keiko Ishii, Toshie Imada, Kosuke Takemura, and Jenny Ramaswamy. "Voluntary Settlement and the Spirit of Independence: Evidence from Japan's 'Northern Frontier.'" *Journal of Personality and Social Psychology* 91, no. 3 (2006): 369–384.

Kleinman, Arthur, Yan Yunxiang, Jing Jun, Lee Sing, Everett Zhang, Pan Tianshu, Wu Fei, Guo Jinhua. *Deep China: The Moral Life of the Person*. Berkeley: University of California Press, 2011.

Knight, Sabina. *Chinese Literature: A Very Short Introduction*. Oxford, New York: Oxford University Press, 2012.

Kundera, Milan. *The Art of the Novel*. New York: Grove Press, 1988.

——. *The Book of Laughter and Forgetting*. Translated by Michael Henry Heim. New York: Knopf, 1980.

Lam, Andrew. "Lessons of Anime—How to Cope With Japan's Tragedy." *New American Media,* March 30, 2011. Available at http://newamericamedia.org/2011/03/lessons-of-anime----how-to-cope-with-japans-tragedy.php

Lee, L. C. "Daycare in the People's Republic of China." In *Child Care in Context: Cross-cultural Perspectives,* edited by A. G. Broberg, C. P. Hwang, M. E. Lamb, and K. J. Sternberg. Hillsdale, N.J.: Lawrence Erlbaum Associates, 1992.

Leightman, Michelle D., Qi Wang, and David B. Pillemere. "Cultural Variations in Interdependence and Autobiographical Memory: Lessons from Korea, China, India, and the United States." In *Autobiographical Memory and the Construction of a Narrative Self,* edited by Robyn Fivush and Catherine A. Haden. Mahwah, N.J.: L. Erlbaum, 2003.

Levine, Lawrence W. *Highbrow/Lowbrow: The Emergence of Cultural Hierarchy in America.* Cambridge, Mass.: Harvard University Press, 1988.

Lightman, Alan. *A Sense of the Mysterious: Science and the Human Spirit.* New York: Pantheon Books, 2005.

Lin Yutang. *My Country and My People.* New York: Reynal and Hitchcock, 1935.

MacLeish, Archibald. *The Collected Poems of Archibald MacLeish.* Boston: Houghton Mifflin, 1962.

Mann, Thomas. *Buddenbrooks.* New York: Knopf, 1964.

Marger, Martin N. *Race and Ethnic Relations: American and Global Perspectives.* Belmont, Calif.: Wadsworth, 1985.

Marshall, Roger. "Variances in Levels of Individualism across Two Cultures and Three Social Classes." *Journal of Cross-Cultural Psychology* 28, no. 4 (1997): 490–495.

McAdams, Dan P. *The Redemptive Self: Stories Americans Live By.* New York: Oxford University Press, 2006.

McCabe, Alyssa, in collaboration with Barbara Burt, Karen Craddock-Willis, Martha D. Crago, Masahiko Minami, Diane Pesco, and Marguerita Jimenez Silva. *Chameleon Readers: Teaching Children to Appreciate All Kinds of Good Stories.* New York: McGraw-Hill, 1996.

McPherson, James Alan. *Crabcakes*. New York: Simon and Schuster, 1998.

Milosz, Czeslaw. *The Collected Poems: 1931–1987*. New York: Ecco Press, 2001.

Miner, Earl. *Comparative Poetics: An Intercultural Essay on Theories of Literature*. Princeton, N.J.: Princeton University Press, 1990.

Musil, Robert. *The Confusions of Young Törless*. Translated by Shaun Whiteside. New York: Penguin, 2001.

Nisbett, Richard E. *The Geography of Thought: How Asians and Westerners Think Differently . . . and Why*. New York: Free Press, 2003.

Orwell, George. *The Orwell Reader*. New York: Harcourt Brace Jovanovich, 1956.

Osnos, Evan. "The Han Dynasty." *New Yorker*, July 4, 2011.

——. "The Unwritten Rules in Chinese Technology." *New Yorker* (online), June 13, 2012. Available at http://www.newyorker.com/online/blogs/evanosnos/2012/06/the-unwritten-rules-in-chinese-technology.html.

Paley, Grace. *Just as I Thought*. New York: Farrar, Straus and Giroux, 1998.

Pamuk, Orhan. *My Name Is Red*. Translated by Erdağ Göknar. New York: Knopf, 2001.

——. *The Naïve and the Sentimental Novelist*. Cambridge, Mass.: Harvard University Press, 2010.

Proust, Marcel. *Swann's Way: In Search of Lost Time,* vol. 1. Translated by Lydia Davis. General editor Christopher Prendergast. New York: Viking, 2003.

Rank, Otto. *Art and Artist: Creative Urge and Personality Development.* New York: Knopf, 1943.

Robinson, Luke. "Alternative Archives and Individual Subjectivities: Ou Ning's *Meishi Street,*" in *Senses of Cinema* (online), July 8, 2012. Available at: http://sensesofcinema.com/2012/63/alternative-archives-and-individual-subjectivities-ou-nings-meishi-street/.

Ross, Michael, and Qi Wang. "Why We Remember and What We Remember: Culture and Autobiographical Memory." *Perspectives on Psychological Science* 5, no. 4 (2010): 402–409.

Shen Fu. *Six Records of a Life Adrift.* Translated by Graham Sanders. Indianapolis: Hackett, 2011.

Shonagon, Sei. *The Pillow Book.* Translated by Meredith McKinney. New York: Penguin Group, 2006.

Silko, Leslie Marmon. "Language and Literature from a Pueblo Indian Perspective." In *Critical Fictions,* edited by Philomena Mariani. Seattle: Seattle Bay Press, 1991.

Sollors, Werner. *Beyond Ethnicity: Consent and Descent in American Culture.* New York: Oxford University Press, 1986.

Sontag, Susan. *Against Interpretation, and Other Essays.* New York: Farrar, Straus and Giroux, 1966.

Strawson, Galen. "Against Narrativity." *Ratio* 17, no. 4 (2004): 428–452.

Tamis-LeMonda, Catherine, Niobe Way, Diane Hughes, Hirokazu Yoshikawa, Ronit Kahana Kalman, and Erika Y. Niwa. "Parents' Goals for Children: The Dynamic Coexistence of Individualism and Collectivism in Cultures and Individuals." *Social Development* 17, no. 1 (2008): 183–209.

Tocqueville, Alexis de. Translated by Arthur Goldhammer. *Democracy in America.* New York: Library of America, 2004.

Trilling, Lionel. *The Opposing Self.* New York: Viking, 1955.

———. *Beyond Culture.* New York: Harcourt Brace Jovanovich, 1978.

Wang, Qi. "Are Asians Forgetful? Perception, Retention, and Recall in Episodic Remembering." *Cognition* 111, no. 1 (2009): 123–131.

———. "Being American, Being Asian: The Bicultural Self and Autobiographical Memory in Asian Americans." *Cognition* 107, no. 2 (2008): 743–751.

———. "Culture and the Development of Self-Knowledge." *Current Directions in Psychological Science* 15, no. 4 (2006): 182–187.

———. "Earliest Recollections of Self and Others in European American and Taiwanese Young Adults." *Current Directions in Psychological Science* 17, no. 8 (2006): 708–714.

———. "The Emergence of Cultural Self-Constructs: Autobiographical Memory and Self-Description in European American and Chinese Children." *Developmental Psychology* 40, no. 1 (2004): 3–15.

——. "Emotion Knowledge and Autobiographical Memory across the Preschool Years: A Cross-Cultural Longitudinal Investigation." *Cognition* 108, no. 1 (2008): 117–135.

Wang, Qi, and Michael Ross. "What We Remember and What We Tell: The Effects of Culture and Self-Priming on Memory Representations and Narratives." *Memory* 13, no. 6 (2005): 594–606.

Wang, Qi, and Michelle D. Leichtman. "Same Beginnings, Different Stories: A Comparison of American and Chinese Children's Narratives." *Child Development* 71, no. 5 (2000): 1329–1346.

Wang, Qi, Michelle Leichtman, and Katherine I. Davies. "Sharing Memories and Telling Stories: American and Chinese Mothers and Their 3-year-olds." *Memory* 8, no. 3 (2000): 159.

Wang, Qi, Yubo Hou, Huizhen Tang, and Alicia Wiprovnick. "Travelling Backwards and Forwards in Time: Culture and Gender in the Episodic Specificity of Past and Future Events." *Memory* 19, no. 1 (2011): 103–109.

Winnicott, D. W. *Playing and Reality.* New York: Basic Books, 1971.

Wood, James. *The Broken Estate: Essays on Literature and Belief.* New York: Random House, 1999.

Wood, Michael. "The Other Case," in *Daedalus,* 141, no. 1 (2012): 130–138.

Woolf, Virginia. *Moments of Being.* Edited by Jeanne Schulkind. New York: Harcourt, 1985.

——. *Mrs. Dalloway.* San Diego: Harvest Harcourt, 1925.

Wu Pei-yi. *The Confucian's Progress: Autobiographical Writings in Traditional China.* Princeton, N.J.: Princeton University Press, 1990.

Xu, Xiaofang. "Familiar and Strange: A Comparison of Children's Literature in Four Cultures." Unpublished manuscript, Eliot-Pearson Department of Child Study, Tufts University, Medford, Mass., 1993.

Yates, Richard. *Revolutionary Road.* Boston: Little, Brown, 1961.

Index

Aesthetics, 99, 116, 118. *See also* Art

African Americans, 38-39, 40-41, 47, 62

Ai Weiwei, 114, 130-131, 175n7

Alcott, Louisa May, *Little Women,* 102, 142

America, 100, 112, 135; cultural hierarchy in, 94; educational ideals in, 48; and fairy tales, 38; and literature, 95; rebirth in, 147-148; and self, 3; in *World and Town,* 154

American colonial diaries, 75, 141

Americans: and autobiography, 75-76, 83-84; and car culture, 7

Architecture, 26, 122, 138

Art, 94, 96; and alienation, 134; as autotelic, 96, 98, 110; and borrowing of landscape, 116; consumerist view of, 135; cultural employment of, 96-97; and cultural hierarchy in America, 94; defamiliarization by, 91; as disinterested, 173n28; Eastern, 76; erotics of, 134; and genius, 76; and independent self, 87; and individualism, 58; and in-

Art *(continued)*
dividuals, 96; interdependent views of, 165n13; and
liberation, 91; as nonin-
strumental, 96; and play,
95; power of, 102; and practice and mastery, 165n13;
and purpose, 2, 90, 99,
170n19; and purposeless
purpose, 95–96, 154, 159;
and sacred spark within,
76, 165n13; and study and
practice, 76; and thinking
outside the box, 91, 154–155;
as useless, 94, 154; visual,
91, 93; Western, 1, 48, 76,
90–91, 94, 96, 154, 159. *See
also* Fiction
Art for art's sake, 76,
170n19
Asian Americans: and epi-
sodic memories, 74, 86;
and episodic specificity, 80;
focused tenacity of, 45; and
group actions, 61; and interpersonal relations, 61;
journal keeping by, 61; life
events recalled by, 64; and
low-elaborative mothers,
86; other-focus of, 61, 62; as

primed for Western vs.
Asian self, 63; as real Americans, 114; self-definition in
relationship to others, 63–
64; self-narratives of, 64;
and uniqueness, 59
Asian-born immigrants, and
self-narratives, 59, 60, 61,
66, 67–69
Asians: autobiographical
writings of, 64; and con-
text, 166n7; danger felt by,
37–38; and episodic spe-
cificity, 80; and figure in
context studies, 69, 71; focused tenacity of, 45; as genetically disposed to
interdependent self, 74; holistic orientation of, 166n7;
journal keeping by, 66–67;
life events recalled by, 64;
and low-elaborative con-
versation, 169n14; and
memory of personal
events, 66; and Nisbett, 60,
74; other-focus of, 62; as
possessing ancient wis-
dom, 71–72; and preference
for intuitive and nonver-
bal, 124; self-definition in

relationship to others, 63–64; self-narratives of, 59, 60, 64; and uniqueness, 59

Asian second-generation immigrants, creativity of, 110–111

Austen, Jane, 1; *Emma*, 171n21; *Pride and Prejudice*, 93, 142–143

Authenticity, 98, 132

Autobiographies, 57, 110; African American, 39; and Americans, 75–76, 83–84; Asian vs. Western, 64; and classical Chinese, 169n16; and Defoe, 82; elaborated, 80; and immigrants, 114; and interdependent cultures, 124; and little emperors study, 73; and Shen Fu, 26–27; Western, 64

Bartlett, Frederic C., *Remembering*, 5–6, 63, 66, 124

Belgium, 75, 139

Bellow, Saul, 134

Biographical Literature (Zhuanji Wenxue), 64

Brain, 64–66, 71

Bruner, Jerome, 72–73

Buddhism, 158

Burt, Ron, 111

Cambodia, 158

Camus, Albert, *The Stranger*, 100–101

Cao Xueqin, *The Story of the Stone*, 131

Car culture, 7, 97

Cardiff, Janet, *The Forty Part Motet*, 156, 157

Cather, Willa, *Song of the Lark*, 143

Catholicism, 134–135

Cervantes, Miguel de, 137; *Don Quixote*, 139, 142

Chang, Joanne, 99–100

Changelings, 4–5

Childhood development, 73–74

Children, 86, 95, 97, 174n3; culture and play of, 86; interdependent vs. independent styles of rearing, 124; as knowing without being told, 125; narratives of, 78, 79; and separation from mother, 173n29. *See also* Mothers

China: and capitalism, 38; and cat-and-mouse games, 129; childhood development in, 73–74; civil service exams in, 45–46; education in, 45–46, 48, 51, 77; government of, 130–131; growing up in, 8; Imperial, 38; Japanese invasion of, 13, 51, 52–53; and self, 3; two-facedness in, 129–130; view of literature in, 95; writers in, 2

Chinese: danger felt by, 37–38; groupishness of, 37–38; hometowns of, 15; and humor, 128–129; and life as stage, 131

Chinese, classical, 83, 97, 169n16

Chinese American writers, 115–116

Chongqing, 51, 52, 103

Chua, Amy, 37, 106; *Battle Hymn of the Tiger Mother,* 48

Civil Rights movement, 113, 115

Collectivity, 3, 7, 60, 97, 117

Communists, 22, 36, 39

Communitarianism, 155

Confucianism, 109, 170n18

Confucius, 3, 51

Context, 7, 116, 118, 155; and Asians, 166n7; envisioned from perspective of others, 61; and Fan Kuan, 90; and hometown, 15; and Norman Jen, 24, 57; and Norman Jen's grandfather, 21–22; questions oriented toward, 135; responsiveness to, 114; and self, 109; and Shen Fu, 27; studies of, 69–71. *See also* Environment; Society

Conversation: high-elaborative style of, 78, 79, 123; low-elaborative style of, 77–78, 86, 110, 169nn13,14. *See also* Mothers

Creativity, 110–111, 112, 159

Cultural Revolution, 12, 38, 125–126

Culture(s), 2–3, 76, 79; and childhood play, 86; and children's narratives, 78; constructions of, 155; employment of art by, 96–97; Geertz on, 72; and hierarchy in America, 94; and interdependent self, 96–97; and inter-/independence spectrum, 8; location between, 111; as mediating self-making, 85; Protestant, Anglo-Saxon, 75, 139; psyche and, 73; with small c vs. large C, 9, 58, 85, 98; and stereotyping, 5; templates of, 7; and writers, 139

Damrosch, David, 85
Daoism, 28, 90, 109, 170n18
Defoe, Daniel, 82
Democracy, 124, 158
Demos, John, *Circles and Lines,* 75, 83–84, 141, 158
Didacticism, 96, 115, 170n19
Digital technology, 117
Double-consciousness, 62
Douglass, Frederick, 39, 40
Drive, 40, 44–45, 47, 101, 111, 132
Du Bois, W. E. B., 62

East, artistic disconnect with West: in literature, 96; and self, 3, 4

Easterners: and episodic memory, 65; and holistic phenomena, 72
Education, 85, 97; in China, 45–46, 48, 51, 77; and interdependence, 165n13; of Agnes Jen, 105; of Norman Jen, 41–44, 45, 47
Egalitarianism, 48
Eliot, George, *Middlemarch,* 138, 142–143
Enlightenment, 85
Environment, 74, 87, 110, 166n7. *See also* Context; Society
Episodic memory. *See* Memory, episodic
Europe, 4, 60, 139, 140
European Americans, 78; and episodic memories, 80, 86; as individualistic, 74; journal keeping by, 61; life events recalled by, 64; narrative event-parsing by, 67–69; self-focus of, 61, 62; and self-narratives, 59–60, 64; and uniqueness, 59

Fairy tales, 38, 39
Family, 15, 33, 34, 135, 154

Family genealogy book, 12–14

Fan Kuan, *Travelers among Mountains and Streams,* 87–90, 97, 98, 109–110, 125, 170n19

Farver, Jo Ann M., 86

Faulkner, William, 115; *Absalom, Absalom!* 143

Fiction, 79–102, 112–113; as civilizing force, 172n24; and episodic specificity, 80–81; internal conflict in, 115; and liberation, 171n22. *See also* Art; Narrative; Novel, the; Writers

Figure-in-context studies, 69–71

Fitzgerald, Robert, 148

Flaubert, Gustave, *Madame Bovary,* 139

Fleet Foxes, "Helplessness Blues," 156

Forbidden City, Beijing, 24–26

Foucault, Michel, 50–51

Freud, Sigmund, 131, 173n28

Geertz, Clifford, 72

Gender, 30–31, 172n23

Genealogical records, 12–14

Germany, 75, 139

Gladwell, Malcolm, 54

Globalization, 4, 155

Grizzly Man, 118

Gross-Loh, Christine, 124

Hamsun, Knut, *Hunger,* 171n21

Han Han, 129–130

Han Dynasty, 45

Hardy, Thomas, 155, 171n20

Harvard University, 46, 48

Hašek, Jaroslav, 140

Heian court, 84

Heian period women, 83

Herzog, Werner, 118

Hessler, Peter, *River Town,* 77, 125

Hierarchy, 48, 50, 94

Hispanic children, 78

Historical impulse, 99

Hokkaido Japanese, 74–75, 110, 167n8

Holdaway, Jennifer, 110–111

Holistic, the, 65, 71, 72, 76, 116, 166n7

Hsu Pao-zao, 32–34

Hsueh Ching-chih, 95

Huángdì (Yellow Emperor), 14

Hughart, Barry, *The Story of the Stone,* 142

Humor, 131–132, 161

Immigrants, 94; and autobiographies, 114; children of, 59; creativity of, 110–111; development of children of, 73–74; return home by, 126; second-generation, 59; and self-narratives, 59, 60

Independence, 102; as balanced with interdependence, 133; and child-rearing styles, 124; and Proust, 82; recent research on, 58; in "The Third Dumpster," 126–128; and values, 80; and Westerners vs. Easterners, 60; in *Who's Irish?* 120–121. *See also* Self, independent

Individuals/individualism, 3, 102, 115, 135; ambivalence about, 155; and American education, 48; and Americans, 75–76; and art, 96; and collective, 117; and European Americans, 59, 74; and Hokkaido Japanese,

74–75; and James, 138, 173n25; and Japanese, 74–75; in "Just Wait," 119–120; and Kundera, 136, 139–140; and making things up, 86; and Nisbett, 4, 60, 75, 139; and the novel, 94; positive vs. negative effects of, 158; priming for, 63; psychological evaluation of, 168n9; slavish celebration of, 98–99; and social change, 73; and Sontag, 135; and uniqueness, 36; and Western art, 58, 76, 90–91; in *World and Town,* 154

Interdependence, 102, 104, 115, 157–158, 161; in adult narratives, 78–79; and art, 76; and autobiographical disinterest, 124; as balanced with independence, 133; basic human comfort in, 126; and child-rearing styles, 124; and Chinese educational system, 48; and Chinese humor, 129; and Chinese two-facedness, 129–130; and connection with nature, 125; and edu-

Individuals/individualism
(*continued*)
cation, 165n13; and epi-
sodic memory, 65; and Fan
Kuan, 89–90; and gender,
172n23; horror and *angst* of
leaving, 125; in "House,
House, Home," 122, 126;
and Hsu Pao-zao, 33; independent terms for phe-
nomena of, 118; and Nor-
man Jen, 11–12, 108–109;
and journal-keeping study,
67; and Kundera, 139, 143;
in linking of polar oppo-
sites, 107; and lower socioeconomic status, 73; and
Proust, 82, 83; recent research on, 58; and social
harmony, 125; in "The
Third Dumpster," 126–128;
variation among countries
of, 75; and Westerners vs.
Easterners, 60; and Yíxīng
teapots, 20–21. *See also* Self,
interdependent
Inter-/independence spec-
trum, 8, 83, 111–112, 139
Interiority, 57, 81, 98, 140, 141

Iowa Writers' Workshop, 112,
113

James, Henry, 137–139,
173n25; *The Art of the Novel*,
135–136; *The Portrait of a
Lady*, 138; *The Wings of the
Dove*, 138
Japan/Japanese, 13, 38, 42, 51,
52–53, 74–75, 78, 83, 103, 110,
167n8
Japanese "I novels"
(*Watakushi shosetsu*), 64
Jen, Agnes, 12, 104–105, 149
Jen, Gish: "House, House,
Home," 121–122, 126; inde-
pendence from parents,
148–149; at Iowa Writers'
Workshop, 112, 113; "Just
Wait," 119–120; *The Love
Wife*, 12, 147; *Mona in the
Promised Land*, 93, 113; read-
ing by, 100–102, 111–112;
"Rewriting the Context,"
114–115; "The Third Dump-
ster," 126–128, 131–132; *Typi-
cal American*, 116, 119, 159,
174n1; *Who's Irish?* 119, 120–
121; *World and Town*, 62, 142,

144–148, 150–154; writing
by, 114–160

Jen, Norman Chao-pe, 149;
and aunt's wedding, 24–26,
49; autobiography of, 8, 9,
11–55, 57, 61, 69, 83, 87, 98,
107–108, 109, 155; character
of, 35–36; and Chen, 45, 47;
danger faced by, 39–40; decision to stay in America,
107–108; desire to become
monk, 28, 165n9; and doors
of family house, 22–24, 26,
27–28; drive of, 40, 44–45;
education of, 41–44, 45, 47;
expectations of, 107; and
family genealogy book, 12–
14; family house of, 15–16,
18, 22–24, 26, 27–28, 120,
129, 140; father of, 34–35;
glass-bottomed pavilion of
family of, 49–50; grandfather of, 13, 15, 16, 17, 18, 21–
22, 29–30, 49, 57; and
grandfather's departure,
36–37, 39; and grandfa-
ther's dream, 39–40; and
grandfather's rooms, 23,
24; grandmother of, 30–32,
35; marriage of, 104–105;
and memories of child-
hood, 35; mother of, 32–35;
name of, 17, 164n3; and National Central University,
45, 47, 51–53, 103; plan to
adopt, 40; and plate-
smashing incident, 35; and
pond, 28; and return to
Yíxīng, 126; sense of chosenness, 40; and Shen Fu,
27; and studies during Japanese invasion, 52–53, 103,
107; as teacher, 54–55, 105–
107, 108–109, 126, 149, 160–
161; watching by, 28–29, 48–
49; work and career of,
53–54; and world of open-
ing and closing doors, 112

Journal-keeping study, 61,
66–67

Joyce, James, *Ulysses,* 140

Kafka, Franz: *The Castle,* 140–
141, 175n7; *Metamorphosis,*
93

Kant, Immanuel, 95, 154,
170n19

Karate Kid, The, 106, 108

Kasinitz, Philip, 110–111
Kingston, Maxine Hong, 115–116; *Woman Warrior,* 174n1
Kitayama, Shinobu, 58, 74
Knight, Sabina, 86
Korean-American preschoolers, 86
Kundera, Milan, 138, 143, 144, 175nn5,6; *The Art of the Novel,* 136–137, 139–142

Lam, Andrew, 38
Lander, Lori, *Girls, Klungkung, Bali,* 126, 127
L'Engle, Madeleine, *A Wrinkle in Time,* 101
Levine, Lawrence, *Highbrow/ Lowbrow,* 93–94, 98
Li Cheng, 90
Liberation, 91, 93, 98–99, 171n22
Lightman, Alan, 6
Lin Yutang, *My Country and My People,* 128–129, 131
Linearity, 30, 53, 64, 75, 76, 79, 98, 148
Literature: in America, 95; Chinese view of, 95; didactic, 96; Eastern, 96; and gender, 172n23; and imitation as innate, 172n24; and independent self, 98, 102; modern, 133; as useful, 95; Western, 102. *See also* Art; Fiction; Novel, the
Little emperors study, 73–74, 78, 110

Ma, Yo-Yo, 12
MacLeish, Archibald, 94–95
Making, 85–86
Mann, Thomas, 132–133, 171n22; *Buddenbrooks,* 133
Marger, Martin M., 5
Markus, Hazel, 58
McAdams, Dan, 38–39
McCabe, Allyssa, *Chameleon Readers,* 78
McPherson, James Alan, 3, 112, 133
Meishi Street, 117–118
Melville, Herman: "Bartleby the Scrivener," 102; *Moby Dick,* 138, 143
Memory, 100, 123–124; episodic, 65–66, 74, 80, 81–82, 86, 98–99, 110, 163n3, 166n3; of life events, 64; and little emperors study, 73–74; and

Native American ghost tale experiment, 6; and priming, 63; and schema, 6; semantic, 65

Metropolitan Museum of Art, 93–94

Milosz, Czeslaw, "Ars Poetica?" 159–160

Miner, Earl, 26–27

Mollenkopf, John, 110–111

Mothers, 85, 97; Chinese, 77; Chinese immigrant, 77; high-elaborative, 78, 79; and inter- or independent self, 76–78; low-elaborative, 77–78, 86. *See also* Children; Conversation

Multiculturalism, 113, 114–115

Museum of Modern Art (New York), performance art in, 91, 92

Musil, Robert, 140; *Confusions of Young Törless,* 173n25

Names, 15–18, 164n3

Narrative, 64; African American, 38–39, 40–41, 47; of children, 78, 79; chosenness, pilgrimage, and redemption pattern in, 39; event-parsing of, 67–69; fascination with Western, 99, 100; and individualism, 58; mainstream American, 39–40; recent research on, 58; and self-construction, 59; and Shen Fu, 27; as sustaining cultural differences, 85; Western, 9, 164n2. *See also* Fiction; Self-narratives

Narrative recall experiment, 5–6, 63, 66

Native American ghost tale experiment, 5–6, 63, 124

Natural, the, 154–155

Nature, 87, 90, 125

Never Sorry, 114

Nietzsche, Friedrich, 173n28

Nisbett, Richard, 4, 60, 61, 72, 74, 75, 139, 168n10

Northern Song Dynasty, 87

Novel, the, 79, 111; as asking forbidden questions, 93; by Chinese Americans, 114; as dead, 159; empathy in, 171n21; and independent self, 93; and individualism, 94, 159; and James, 135–136, 137–139; Kundera on, 136–

Novel *(continued)*
137; and liberation, 98–99;
and Milosz, 159–160; as
questioning, 95. *See also*
Art; Fiction; Narrative

Orwell, George, "Why I
Write," 99
Other-focus, 61, 62, 67
Ou Ning, 117

Paley, Grace, 95
Pamuk, Orhan, 143–144; *My
Name Is Red,* 144
Perception, 64–65, 66–67,
69–72
Play, 48, 95, 96, 97, 159
Poetry, 85–86, 94–95
Priming experiment, 63, 66
Proulx, Annie, "Brokeback
Mountain," 93
Proust, Marcel, 86, 97, 140,
141; *In Search of Lost Time,*
81–83, 98
Pueblo Indian folktales, 79
Purpose, 135
Purposelessness, 90, 170n19
Purposeless purpose, 95–96,
154, 159

Qing Dynasty, 24

Rank, Otto, 95
Reading, 102, 111–112
Relationships, 63–64, 67, 72,
78, 109
Robinson, Luke, 116–118

Salinger, J. D., *Catcher in the
Rye,* 155
Sanders, Graham, 27
Scarsdale, New York, 100
Self: American, 147–148; confrontational, 60; construction of, 58, 59–60; and context, 109; as contingent
affair, 141; and culture, 85;
different constructions of,
2–9; diminution of, 109;
and Enlightenment, 85;
false vs. true, 148; inter-/
independent, 142; in Kafka,
141; in Kundera, 141–142;
liberation of, 171n22; modern Western, 85; naviga-
tory, 60, 170n19; premod-
ern, 141; priming for, 63;
questioning of delimited,
141

Self, independent, 3–5; and art, 87; as cultural construction, 155; and episodic memory, 65–66, 110; and episodic specificity, 80; fiction as sanctuary of, 113; and inherent attributes, 7; and making, 85; and mothers, 76–78; movement from interdependent self toward, 147; need for, 158–159; and the novel, 93; and passivity, 60–61; as reinforced and policed, 97–98; and rights and self-expression, 3; and Sontag, 135; as term, 6–7; and uniqueness, 7; and Western literature, 102; and Western narrative, 9; and Winnicott, 173n29; and Woolf, 123; in *World and Town*, 147. *See also* Independence

Self, interdependent, 3–5; 166n7; and affiliation, duty, and self-sacrifice, 3; Asians as genetically disposed to, 74; and classical Chinese, 83; and commonality, 7; and context, 7; as cultural construction, 155; and culture, 96–97; and Norman Jen, 8, 57, 109; joy in, 121; loss of, 121; and memory, 65; and mothers, 76–78; need for, 158–159; and passivity, 60; and place, roles, loyalties, and duties, 7; as term, 7; in *Who's Irish?* 121; in *World and Town*, 147. *See also* Interdependence

Self-focus, 60, 62, 66–67

Self-narratives, 59–60, 61, 64, 65, 66, 67–69. *See also* Narrative

Shakespeare, William: *Hamlet*, 3; *King Lear*, 35, 108

Shame, 107, 108, 125–126

Shandong Coal Mining Institute, 103, 104

Shanghai, 19, 36, 42

Shen Fu, *Six Records of a Life Adrift*, 26–27, 29, 64, 115, 141

Shikibu, Murasaki, *Tale of Genji*, 84

Shim, Yoolim Lee, 86

Shonagon, Sei, *The Pillow Book*, 84, 97, 110

Shweder, Richard, 73
Silko, Leslie Marmon, 79
Singaporeans, 69, 71, 109, 120
Social class, 37–38, 73
Social constructions, 154–155
Social role, 21, 29, 57
Society: confrontation of, 93, 94; resistance to, 98. *See also* Context; Environment
Sollors, Werner, 3
Song Dynasty, 45, 87, 98
Sontag, Susan, 134–135
Soviet Bloc, 140
Stauffer, John, 2, 57, 104, 155
Sterne, Lawrence, 137
Strawson, Galen, 157
Structural hole, 111, 133
Stuyvesant High School, New York, 47

Tàihú (Lake Tai), 19–20
Tallis, Thomas, *Spem in alium,* 157
Thoreau, Henry David, "History of Himself," 76
Tocqueville, Alexis de, 75
Tolstoi, Leo, *War and Peace,* 138

Trilling, Lionel, 93, 132–133, 171n20; *Beyond Culture,* 171n22

Uniqueness, 7, 17; and European Americans, 59; and individualism, 36; and Kundera, 139–140; and Norman Jen, 57; and Norman Jen's grandfather, 22; priming for, 63; and Sontag, 135
Updike, John, 134

Venice Biennale, 91
Voice, 132, 158

Wang, Qi, 58–59, 61, 62–63, 66–69, 76–77, 80, 85, 100, 159
Waters, Mary, 110–111
Watt, Ian, *The Rise of the Novel,* 82, 136
Wells, H. G., 137–138
West/Westerners: and discoveries involving discrete objects, 72; and episodic memory, 65; and figure in context studies, 69, 71; and

logic and categorization, 72; and Nisbett, 4, 60, 72, 74; priming of, 63; and self, 3, 4; writers in, 1-2. *See also* Art

Wharton, Edith, *The House of Mirth,* 142, 143

Wood, James, 79

Wood, Michael, 157

Woolf, Virginia, 81, 86; *Moments of Being,* 79-80; *Mrs. Dalloway,* 122-123

World Journal, 149

World War II, 103, 104

Wright, Richard, *Native Son,* 143

Writers, 132; and culture, 9, 139; separatism of, 134

Writing, 61-62; reasons for, 1-2, 99; as subversive, 92, 114. *See also* Fiction; Narrative; Novel, the

Wu Pei-yi, *The Confucian's Progress,* 83

Yates, Richard, *Revolutionary Road,* 133

Yíxīng, 18-20, 36, 37, 108, 126, 129; teapots from, 20-21